Teaching Excellence

A Field Guide
For Coaching and Developing
Novice Teachers

yesprep

Teaching Excellence: A Field Guide For Coaching and Developing Novice Teachers

YesPrep

Published by YES Prep Public Schools

For ordering information or special discounts for bulk purchases, please contact teaching.excellence@yesprep.org

Design and composition by Daniel Ruesch Design, Inc. www.danielruesch.net.

Kendra Young, editor

ISBN: 978-0-692-94194-2
First Edition
First printing: August 2018

Contents

ACKNOWLEDGMENTS 9

FORWARD 11

INTRODUCTION 15

   Core Beliefs 16

   Why This Book 17

   Why Teaching Excellence 18

   How to Read This Book 18

CHAPTER 1 **The Teacher Educator** 21

   Mindsets 22

   TE Rubric Tiers 1-4 25

CHAPTER 2 **Building Teacher Relationships** 27

   First Steps 28

   Establish a Connection 30

   Set Expectations 32

   On the Journey 33

CHAPTER 3 **Building Stakeholder Relationships** 39

   The Power of Partners 39

   First Steps 41

   First Meeting 41

   Check-Ins 42

   Next Steps 44

   Wrap Up: Staying on Course 45

CHAPTER 4 **Organizational Skills**................................47

Making Time 48

Tracking Time 50

Staying Current...................................52

Fitting It All In...................................52

Tracking Communications and Status................53

Tracking Touchpoints..............................53

And the Rest......................................54

CHAPTER 5 **Observing the Classroom** 57

Before You Walk In 57

Establishing an Objective...........................57

Advance Notice...................................60

In the Room 60

Capturing Notes 60

Capturing Student Data............................62

Intervening.......................................66

On Your Way Out 66

After You Leave...................................67

CHAPTER 6 **Identifying a Key Lever** 69

Understanding Levers 69

Based on a Rubric 70

Developmentally Appropriate 71

Grounded in Student Data..........................72

Identifying Levers.................................73

Observation 74

Instinct 74

Suitability.......................................75

Choosing Between Multiple Key Levers 75

CHAPTER 7 **Flow of a Debrief** 77

Purpose and Outcomes 79

Structure..79

Build the Relationship 80

Logistics 81

Glow 82

Transfer 83

Grow 84

Application and Practice 85

Closing 85

Appendix: Coaching Conversation Tools 85

Debrief Agenda 86

Coaching Conversation Planner 89

CHAPTER 8 **Criteria for Success** 91

Steps 92

Checklist of Attributes 94

Guiding Questions 95

Coaching with Criteria for Success 95

CHAPTER 9 **Application and Practice** 99

Elements of Application and Practice 99

The Criteria for Success 99

The Model 100

CHAPTER 10 **Additional Considerations During a Debrief** 105

Coaching Considerations 105

Teacher Considerations 112

Going Forward 114

CHAPTER 11 **Alternate Touchpoints** 117

Video Observation 117

Focus Lesson 119

Co-observation 120

Mindset Conversation 121

Real-time Coaching 123

Classroom Reset 126

Research Integration 127

Reflective Practitioner 130

CHAPTER 12 **Lesson Planning Touchpoints** 133

Identifying the Need 134

Planning the Conversation 135

Executing the Conversation. 136

Observing the Results. 136

Areas of Focus 137

Scope and Sequence 137

Specific Section 137

CHAPTER 13 **Data-driven Coaching**. 141

What Data to Integrate 143

Data for Non-Traditional Subjects 145

Data Dives 146

Types of Data. 149

Weekly Quizzes and Unit Assessments. 150

Following Up. 151

CHAPTER 14 **Following Up on the Debrief** 155

When to Follow-up. 155

Types of Follow-up 158

CHAPTER 15 **Coaching Support Staff** 161

Lay the Groundwork 161

Bridge the Gap. 164

Set the Stage 165

Summer Professional Development. 165

Adapt 166

Professional Development 167

Appendix: Special Education Arc of Development 169

CHAPTER 16 **The Professional Learning Core Beliefs**. 171

Professional Learning Must Create Change 171

Professional Learning Sets a Tone 172

Elements of Exemplary Professional Learning Sessions. 172

Continuously Improve. 173

CHAPTER 17 **Creating a Scope and Sequence**. 177

Who Creates a Scope and Sequence and When 178

How to Create a Scope and Sequence 178

Sample Scope and Sequence 180

CHAPTER 18 **Session Writing** 185

Elements of a Session 185

Share the Load...186

Creating a Session 187

CHAPTER 19 **Session Revising and Editing**....................195

Revising vs. Editing 195

Revising 196

Session Checklist...198

Roles and Responsibilities..................................200

Timeline 200

CHAPTER 20 **Internalizing a Session** 203

Excellence is Not an Accident 203

The Internalization Process 204

CHAPTER 21 **Facilitating a Session** 207

Teaching Excellence Facilitation Excellence Rubric...............208

CHAPTER 22 **Developing Facilitators** 217

Program Structure..217

Professional Learning Onboarding 217

Group Sessions 218

One-on-one Coaching......................................218

CLOSING THOUGHTS 221

Acknowledgments

While we have had the privilege of writing this book over the past two years, this project has been the compilation of the hard work of many individuals over the course of well over a decade. First and foremost, we would like to thank Ashley Harris for her role as content editor for chapters on instructional coaching. Her guidance in all phases of writing has been instrumental, and her knowledge of instructional coaching is profound.

Any project of this size needs champions at the earliest stages. Michael Warburton believed this book could help educators (and thus students) in a meaningful way and helped us ensure it could get off the ground when we were in need of dedicated, talented people. Our organization's CEO, Mark DiBella, and our Executive Vice President of Strategy & Advancement Ann Ziker also believed in this project from the start and provided their respective expertise at critical times.

Carlos Villagrana, our Managing Director, and Nella Garcia Urban, our Vice President of Talent, helped to ensure that the vision we had for this book came to fruition while staying true to our program's strengths. Daya Cozzolino Fulton provided content editing for the chapters on Professional Learning.

Karin Espinosa, Rachel Duke, JoAnna Duncan, Andrew McDermott, Maranda Rushing, Christopher Reid, Amara Mattingly, Sarah Murphy Traylor, Jamie Horton, and Lindsay Woodruff each drafted outlines of chapters that became valuable resources as this book came together.

Kyrlyn Chatten, Calvin Stocker, Natalie Lund, Stephanie Kaplun, Isabella Maldonado, Pegah Taylor, and Catlin Goodrow served as our first readers and provided invaluable feedback on an early draft of this book. Channelle Figueroa's expertise in communications and project management were always incredibly insightful.

This book would not have been possible without the financial backing of the Walton Family Foundation. They believe in both the work that YES Prep's Teaching Excellence does, and in the necessity of publishing this book.

Finally, we want to acknowledge the work of all team members past and present. All Instructional Coaches who have worked with Teaching Excellence have impacted the content of these pages and are the collective giants on whose shoulders we stand.

Ashley Dalton
Colin O'Neal
Paul Needham

Forward

In 1999, I became a fifth-grade teacher, assigned as a Teach For America corps member to teach in an underserved community in Houston, Texas. I was convinced that I found the calling of my life's work and have been working in public education ever since. Over those years, the single greatest professional development I have received was from my instructional coach towards the end of my first semester teaching.

For the first three months of my teaching career, my coach visited my classroom every week. Sometimes I knew he was coming ahead of time. Other times, he showed up unannounced. Every time he was there, we were a team learning the art and science of teaching together. My students were our students.

The debrief sessions after his observations were consistent, predictable, and always actionable. I never felt threatened in those meetings, yet complacency was never an option. Over those first months of my career, due in large part to the unwavering commitment of my coach to build a strong personal relationship with me, I trusted him that I was developing as a teacher, that my students were growing, and that there were more things going well than there were areas for improvement.

Then at a visit towards the end of my first semester, everything changed. We had our weekly debrief as usual, but the conversation started in an entirely new way.

"Mark, do you realize that you have a strong bias towards your male students—especially in your math and science classes?"

I will never forget the sting of those words. Defensiveness swelled in me. I felt betrayed; believing I had been wronged, I began to formulate my response—a litany of reasons for why this unfounded statement simply was not true. Before I could launch my counterattack, my coach followed this assertion by pulling from his backpack and placing in front of me three months' worth of data from his observations—page after page where he had noted both my physical presence in the room as well as who I was calling on to answer questions and the depth of the questions I was asking.

There were maps of my classroom that showed where I spent the majority of my time. There were rosters of my students that showed how often I had called on each student, and each question I had asked was tagged with a number 1 through 6 to indicate its corresponding level on Bloom's Taxonomy. The data was incontrovertible. I called on my male students six times more often than I called on my female students, and I asked them higher-order questions four times more often.

The very first time my coach observed me, he correctly intuited that my biggest challenge as a first-year teacher would not be classroom management or keeping up with systems like classroom job assignments. The greatest battle that I would face would not be with an angry parent or an obstinate student. It would be in the harshest battlefield we each confront—our mind and the subconscious limits we assign to the students we are privileged to teach. He saw the early signs of a deep gender bias in my instruction and set out to systematically expose it for the sake of my practice and for the sake of the children I had been entrusted to serve.

Good coaches highlight areas of growth for those they coach. Great coaches inspire change born out of those areas for improvement, but I did not have a good coach or even a great coach. I had an exceptional coach. Exceptional coaches risk much to illuminate invisible roadblocks—barriers to transformational change—and then commit to being a part of that change.

My coach knew that my greatest area for growth would be nearly impossible for me to grasp and harder still for me to change. He knew the only hope for change was through establishing a relationship of trust and accountability with me, coupling that relationship with sound advice grounded in data, and then committing to walking the long road to transformational change with me.

This type of exceptional coaching is where exceptional teaching starts. In my estimation, we far too often attribute greatness to raw talent, yet raw talent is oft squandered. Had I been left to develop on my own as a teacher, I would have likely never confronted the gender bias that reigned my classroom. I would have continued to consider myself a far better teacher than I was. In short, I would have squandered my talent, but my coach would not allow that to happen. For him, the achievement of my students was the ultimate measure of our success, and he was willing to push me to ensure that, for the sake of my students, I became the teacher they deserved.

For the last decade, I have watched with pride as Teaching Excellence has built a cadre of exceptional coaches who, like my coach, stop at nothing to ensure that their students are given every opportunity to flourish.

This book is the power of my coach, a power that has played out in hundreds of Teaching Excellence coaching relationships, translated into practical wisdom and best practices on the pages that follow. But make no mistake. Whether you are an instructional leader seeking to become stronger at coaching or a teacher seeking to better serve your students, this book alone will not change you.

Transformational change, the type of change your students deserve, requires you to take what you read in the chapters that follow and allow yourself to be changed. Even that might not be enough. Like me, you might need to do battle with your mind—forcing yourself to examine whether you have artificially capped the potential of the children you directly or indirectly serve. Your imaginations for your students, lofty as you perceive them to be, are not the ceiling on their ability.

My hope is that through the pages of this book, through the exploration of the pressure tested Teaching Excellence strategies, and through your own deep commitment to developing the art and science of teaching and coaching, you will become an educator who will stop at nothing to ensure that your students receive the world-class education they deserve. This is the path of exceptional educators.

Mark DiBella
CEO
YES Prep Public Schools

Introduction

"A ship in harbor is safe – but that is not what ships are built for."

—John A. Shedd

Think back to your first day in the classroom. How prepared did you feel? How confident? Anxious? As that first day turned into your first week, then into your first month, how did those initial feelings change? How did those emotions fluctuate across the first semester, and ultimately your first year? Many new teachers experience a roller coaster of highs and lows as they encounter a range of student-related successes and challenges that first year; it's all part of the growth process to becoming a stronger educator. Keeping this perspective is crucial to the successful implementation of strategies presented in these pages. The following exercise is intended to prompt reflection on your own experiences as a novice teacher, through the lens of your current role: a teacher educator.

Introductory Reflection Exercise	
What supports that you received as a first-year teacher that were the most helpful? What actions did your supervisors and/or mentor take to develop your knowledge, skills, and mindsets?	What supports do you wish you had received as a first-year teacher? What actions did your supervisors and/or mentor take that left you feeling frustrated, confused, or wanting more support? Was there inaction in any particular part of your development?
Take a moment to answer these questions. Write them down, discuss them with a colleague, or simply reflect on them in the quietness of your own mind.	

If you are someone who had a lot of specific examples from the first column, then you had a strong support system from your campus, district, or teacher preparation program. You will likely be able to draw on many of the strategies your educators used to guide you through the early part of your classroom career; this book will help you sharpen those skills to an even finer, more impactful point. However, if you had more examples from the second column, or your experiences were a mixed bag, then this book will not only help you hone your existing teacher-support toolkit but will also give you coaching techniques that will make you wish for a time machine to travel back and support yourself.

An additional challenge teacher educators face is the need to shift mindsets. As an educator, you are ingrained with the mindset to make decisions based on what is best for students. As teacher educator, decisions about what is best for students must necessarily include teachers; they are now your agents of change in the school. Good leaders prioritize developing and supporting teachers. Consequently, that development in instruction and classroom culture will have the greatest impact on students. The initial transition from a teaching role (where you directly interact with students every day) to an instructional leadership position can be difficult. However, reinforcing teachers' value and putting yourself in their shoes when making instructional decisions will have the greatest holistic impact on the school.

Many times, well-intentioned teacher educators will maintain the same intense focus on student outcomes as they had in the classroom. As a result, sometimes teachers can feel unvalued or unsupported because they feel like a means to an end rather than a partner in driving student achievement. Teachers need to know that you have their back and are devoted to them being successful so that students can be successful.

Teaching can be demanding and stressful job, especially in the early days. Teachers need to see that your belief and support of them is constant even when their performance is poor or inconsistent. This does not mean that you will not hold them accountable, but they do need to understand that your main priority is helping them to be successful teachers in their classrooms.

Core Beliefs

We've designed our program according to a few key philosophies. Though these beliefs are not an explicit part of the way we train our coaches, they are at the heart of our institutional culture, woven throughout a coach's experience, and shared by everyone in our organization. These beliefs drive our success with teachers and our impact on students, and they are the foundation for this book.

Key Philosophies

Teacher educators are agents of change. Our entry point for affecting change in classrooms is through strong teacher educators. That term broadly applies to people who support, evaluate, coach and develop novice teachers. We believe that these people can have a profound impact on a teacher's growth and trajectory, and therefore also impact the quality of learning for students. At TE, we call our teacher educators "instructional coaches," so these two terms will be used interchangeably throughout the book. These terms refer to grade-level chairs, content leaders, district staff, campus administrators, interventionists, and anyone who helps novice teachers grow.

New teachers develop skills along a predictable trajectory. Teaching Excellence has taken the tool used to evaluate teachers at YES Prep, called the Instructional Excellence Rubric, and prioritized it in the order that we believe teachers build their skills. You may use a different evaluation tool, but the same idea applies: teachers build skills in a certain order. During the summer, we focus on the basics of classroom culture and lesson planning. (Our initial coaching touchpoints are also focused solely on these areas.) As teachers master the basics, they move on to higher-level skills. We ask our teachers to focus on only one or two new skills at a time. In our experience, that leads to the most sustained results for teachers as they gradually build their practice while relying on the skills they already have.

Coaching is best done through strong personal relationships. Teacher educators primarily affect change through influence, and that can't be done without a high level of trust. A teacher educator needs to know the teacher personally—and have broad context for their classroom—in order to know the best strategies or actions to recommend. Teachers have to be able to be vulnerable and authentic in classroom observations and coaching sessions so that they can receive the support they most need, rather than feeling like they have to put on a show when someone comes in the room. The connection between a teacher and his or her coach accelerates the teacher's growth and provides a more enjoyable experience for all involved.

Data is central to teaching and coaching. When our teacher educators observe classrooms, they are looking specifically at student outcomes, both academic and behavioral. Those outcomes then point them in the direction of a specific teacher action that needs to change. Coaches also build that same skill in teachers so they can continue to improve after the one year that they spend in Teaching Excellence. Teachers must have an eye for in-the-moment data from student performance, and also the skills to analyze trends in exit tickets, weekly quizzes, unit assessments, and larger assessments.

New teachers must practice skills before they are expected to use them in a classroom. Practice and application are critical components of our program. We spend the bulk of both coaching meetings and professional learning sessions on teacher practice. We ask teachers to stand and deliver routines, expectations, and parts of a lesson in front of their peers during the summer. When coaching, we routinely model or role-play to give teachers practice with a new skill. Teaching is incredibly difficult, and it is hard to flawlessly execute a skill the first time you use it. The best time to try, fail, and try again is in front of a teacher educator—not in front of students.

Why This Book

The single greatest predictor of student achievement is the quality of the teacher, and quality teachers take time to develop. Teacher burn-out is a problem facing every district in the country, and particularly impacts teachers during their first year in the classroom. Teachers frequently cite a lack of support in the classroom as a reason for leaving the profession. This is a waste—not only of the enormous resources school districts pour into teacher development, but also of the opportunity to build a truly excellent teacher at the peak of his or her motivation and excitement for the work. The people with the greatest access to teachers in their first year—their coaches, evaluators, grade-level chairs, and content leaders—are often given this role with little to no targeted development. This book aims to help those people, referred to here interchangeably as "teacher educators" and "coaches," set up systems for impactful instructional coaching that we think will retain and improve teachers in the classroom.

Why Teaching Excellence

Teaching Excellence is a long-standing teacher development organization that has refined its coaching model for more than 12 years. Our success is proven with teachers and coaches alike. Our teachers have won major awards including three Texas Alternative Certification Association Intern of the Year Award winners, and TE alums who have remained strong in the classroom to earn Kinder Excellence in Teaching awards. Our coaches are frequently promoted to administrative roles at campuses where they thrive. We have built strong partnerships with school districts around Houston who believe in our model. Because of the fierce need for improved teacher support and development for the sake of our students, we feel now is the time to start helping others replicate our success.

How to Read This Book

We want you to get the most out of this book to improve yourself, your school, or your organization.

The book is split roughly into two parts. The first begins with the organizational and relational skills needed by great coaches, and then dives deeper into the components of an excellent coaching interaction from beginning to end; including how to identify a key lever to coach, collect data, and structure the coaching conversation. The second section focuses on Teaching Excellence's view of professional learning, which supports coaching and vice versa. The way we write and facilitate sessions catalyzes teacher development and provides a foundation for coaching interactions.

We have been onboarding and coaching novice educators at the beginning of their teaching journey for well over a decade now. In that time, we have learned from many mistakes and, over time, have refined a set of best practices for working with novice educators that have been incredibly successful. We have purposefully set it up as a guidebook, with small chapters. All aligned resources are contained within the chapters where they are introduced. While you may read this book cover to cover once, we hope that sections and pages become dog-eared as you reference specific chapters when they are most useful to you. We also hope you will experience renewed energy for coaching and developing novice teachers and that this text will play a small part in the career educators you mold in the coming years. This work is incredibly challenging and, while sometimes replete with setbacks, is also some of the most important and rewarding work in the field of education. If this sounds like a challenge you're prepared to engage with alongside us, let's leave the harbor!

1

The Teacher Educator

You probably believe, like we do, that setting high standards for students begins with high standards for teachers, administrators, and all other stakeholders in each student's education. At YES Prep, we have codified this belief in a variety of systems driven by a key word: excellence.

It would be insufficient, however, to simply rely on a textbook definition for this term, as excellence manifested in practice can be quite a subjective measure. To establish a clear vision for what excellent teaching is, YES has developed its own rubric – the Instructional Excellence Rubric (IER). This rubric is used on every YES Prep campus as an evaluation of teacher performance, and also as a critical tool for guiding teacher development. A rubric is one of the foundational tools of the teacher educator.

Whether you use a rubric developed by your district or one created by your state's teacher appraisal system, it is paramount to become familiar the scope and sequence of teacher skills and actions. Novice teachers need to know what specific expectations to meet, and one of your primary roles as a coach is to guide them towards meeting those expectations. We recommend you take the internalization of your rubric a step further and tier it based on the developmental needs of novice teachers. At Teaching Excellence, we have done just that to create the TE Rubric. This rubric is a tiered version of the IER; it contains all the same classroom culture elements, planning practices, and lesson delivery components as the standard IER format, but prioritizes them based on which specific skills a novice teacher needs to develop first. For example, Tier 1 emphasizes classroom culture development, the establishment of routines, and the basics of lesson planning, whereas Tier 3 focuses on more advanced lesson planning and delivery skills such as designing rigorous learning experiences and honing questioning strategies.

Teachers are not the only ones who can benefit from a guiding rubric. Teaching Excellence has synthesized more than a decade's worth of coaching expertise into the Instructional Coaching Excellence Rubric (ICER). This rubric is used to evaluate and develop coaches of all experience levels (and can be found at the end of this chapter).

The skills we'd like coaches to develop first include building relationships with teachers, structuring and focusing a debrief (a coaching meeting, usually following an observation), and ensuring that coaching conversations emphasize application and practice. As you read through the language of the ICER, you can probably identify how these skills, as well as the core beliefs discussed in this introduction, manifest in our daily coaching practices.

Mindsets

At Teaching Excellence (TE) we believe in developing talent, that of our teachers and for those who coach teachers. Consistently, we have found that the best coaches are people with passion for teaching and developing others to excel in teaching. In addition to our introductory beliefs and the specific actions outlined in the Instructional Coaching Excellence Rubric, we believe there are certain mindsets that effective teacher educators have in common.

Growth

A teacher with a growth mindset sees feedback on their performance as a catalyst for change and improvement; from his perspective, the person providing feedback is making an investment in their development. Consequently, that educator values and seeks feedback to the point that they ask questions about how to improve and invites follow-up conversations.

Listening to an explanation about how you could have done something better can be painful, but a growth mindset assures you that the positive long-term change is worth the temporary discomfort.

Empathy

The best teacher educators realize that relationships are vital to the work we do. They look for opportunities to understand the life stories of their teachers and value the experiences each teacher brings to the work. Teaching is hard (but rewarding) work, and teacher educators know that teachers need a coach, advocate, trainer, counselor, and cheerleader along the way to become the instructors their students need and deserve.

Often work relationships are characterized by a degree of distance, but you can't mold a life from a distance. Teacher educators realize that if they are to be a catalyst for change, they must engage with their teachers and allow themselves to be touched and moved by their lives. To that end, they invest in building relationships and learning how to influence others, as well as how to push or pull without leaving a bruise.

Adaptability

While we might understand why customer-support call centers force their agents to follow a script, we have all felt the frustration of being forced to go through a set of questions that don't apply to our situation.

The best teacher educators, like the best teachers, understand that we cannot systematize every interaction. We're not dealing with a lost credit card; we're dealing with individuals joined together in one of the most significant and powerful enterprises on the planet—guiding lives, young and old, toward mastery and success.

Teacher educators take the time to listen and understand, to improvise, adapt, and overcome. Teachers need this demonstration of adaptability, not only for the sake of their own development, but as a model for how they can apply this mindset to their classrooms.

Agents of Change

At YES Prep, and for many of the partnership districts supported by Teaching Excellence, the students are primarily students of color and/or from low-income backgrounds. It is critical that teacher educators believe that all students deserve an excellent education, including the opportunity to make it to and through college. However, many schools with the greatest number of challenges are staffed with the highest numbers of inexperienced teachers.

If it is to be, it is up to me.

The best teacher educators see themselves as change agents for teachers and believe that when they gather the right people to focus on a challenge, we can collectively improve student achievement. Effective teacher educators are able to see the educational injustices that exist and are willing to step in to develop teachers to tilt these injustices. It is our job to transform novice teachers into highly effective educators at our school.

1. Why did you transition from classroom instruction to being a teacher educator? What invigorates you about this work? Who is another teacher educator that you would like to emulate?

2. Look at the evaluative rubric used by your campus or district. Which of the skills do you feel are most critical for a new teacher to master early in the year?

3. Reading through the skills outlined in the ICER, which bullets describe coaching practices that you currently do well? What are some growth areas you have based on this tool?

teaching excellence

Teaching Excellence Program
Instructional Coaching Excellence Rubric
(ICER)

IC:			Initial Reflection
Manager:			•
Teacher:			
Date of Shadowing (obs and debrief):			
Date of Debrief (of the debrief):			

Vision of a TEacher

Excellent Instructional Coaching, as articulated by the Instructional Coaching Excellence Rubric, will result in a teacher who exemplifies the following characteristics:

- A successful TEacher understands that the teacher is the single biggest factor in the classroom and ***owns*** that responsibility.
- A successful TEacher is student-centered and data-driven.
- A successful TEacher is a self- aware, reflective practitioner who takes initiative for his/her continuous improvement.

Glows	Grows

Tier I				
	Not Meeting Expectations	**Approaching Proficiency**	**Proficient**	**Mastery**
Building Transformative Relationships	• The coach does not employ active listening strategies. • Mutual respect and trust are not evident. • The teacher's current personal and professional circumstances are not addressed or considered. • The coach does not identify the novice teacher's strengths.	• The coach sometimes employs active listening strategies (adopting teacher language, paraphrasing teacher's thoughts, think time before responding) with mixed success. • Mutual respect and trust are evident in the interactions between the coach and novice teacher at times (tone, body language, vulnerability, risk taking, honest exchange). At other times, the novice teacher may demonstrate a lack of respect for and/or a trust for the coach or the coach may demonstrate a lack of respect for and/or trust of the teacher. • The teacher's current personal and professional circumstances are addressed but not considered when developing action steps. • The coach identifies the novice teacher's strengths, though connections between these strengths and focus areas are not always made clear.	• The coach employs active listening strategies (adopting teacher language, paraphrasing teacher's thoughts, think time before responding) in order to better understand the teacher's perspective and increase teacher investment in the conversation. • Mutual respect and trust are consistently evident in the interactions between the coach and novice teacher (tone, body language, vulnerability, risk taking, honest exchange). • The coach has or is developing a broad context for the teacher's current personal and professional circumstances, and that context is considered when developing action steps. • The coach recognizes and reinforces the novice teacher's strengths and uses these strengths as leverage points to impact focus areas (transfer).	**In addition to the criteria listed in the proficiency column,** • The teacher engages in conversation in a way that indicates buy-in (adds in own ideas, tweaks suggestions to fit specific classroom and student context). • The teacher recognizes his or her own strengths and/or focus areas and as a result is motivated to collaborate around implementation of feedback. • There is evidence that the novice teacher has implemented prior action steps.
Structure/Focus	• The structure of the meeting is consistently unclear, and the structure of the meeting lacks critical components. • The outcome of the meeting is unclear. The meeting often loses focus on the outcome (conversation includes multiple tangents). • Language from the TE Rubric is not referenced. • The meeting lacks pacing to the point that the outcome is not achieved.	• The structure of the meeting is at times unclear and/or is lacking necessary components. • The outcome of the meeting is not explicitly stated. • The meeting sometimes loses focus on the outcome (conversation includes tangents). • The specific language of the TE Rubric is rarely referenced during the meeting. • The meeting occasionally lacks pacing (i.e. too many focus areas, some parts of the conversation are not fully developed, focus area is low impact, too much or too little time spent on any one part of the meeting) which minimizes the impact on teacher action and student outcomes.	• The meeting has a clear and purposeful structure and includes all necessary components. • The outcome of the meeting is explicitly stated. • The meeting remains focused on the outcome. • The specific language of the TE Rubric is referenced throughout the meeting. • The meeting is paced in such a way that the right amount of material pertaining to the outcome is covered, in order to impact teacher action and student outcomes.	**In addition to the criteria listed in the proficiency column,** • The meeting has a clear outcome and the coach incorporates teacher input in referring to that outcome regularly. • The coach significantly modifies the structure of the meeting to address the specific needs of the teacher.

Application	• Criteria for success are not stated. • During the meeting, the coach does not provide examples or model the criteria for success or does so unsuccessfully. • The novice teacher does not have the opportunity to apply the criteria for success. • The coach and teacher do not discuss potential obstacles. • A specific timeline to implement the criteria for success is not suggested and the coach's follow-up is not articulated.	• Criteria for success are either not specific, not clear, or not directly aligned to the outcome. • During the meeting, the coach attempts to provide examples of the criteria for success and/or models the criteria for success with mixed results. • The novice teacher has limited opportunities to apply the criteria for success and/or does not receive specific and strategic feedback. • The coach and teacher discuss potential obstacles without reaching a resolution. • A specific timeline to implement the criteria for success is not suggested and/or the coach's follow-up is not articulated.	• Criteria for success are specific, clear, and directly aligned to the outcome. • During the meeting, the coach provides meaningful examples of the criteria for success and/or successfully models the criteria for success as appropriate. • The novice teacher has ample opportunities to apply the criteria for success and receives specific and strategic feedback. • In order to ensure implementation, the coach and teacher discuss potential obstacles and problem solve in order to mitigate these obstacles. • The coach and/or teacher suggests a timeline to implement the criteria for success. The coach's follow-up is articulated.	**In addition to the criteria listed in the proficiency column,** • The process for implementing the action steps is made explicit such that the teacher will be able to replicate the underlying skill with confidence.

Tier II

Direct Tone and Language	• The coach does not use direct language, compelling rationale, or relevant data. • Tone used in conversation is combative, disrespectful, and/or not the appropriate level of urgency for the conversation. • If the teacher offers pushback, the coach does not address it or does so inappropriately. • The coach does not use wait time to allow for teacher processing (consistently interrupts teachers, answers own questions)	• The coach uses indirect language or data that is at times unclear or misaligned. • At times, the coach uses a tone that is not confident or assertive (fillers, uptalk). • If the teacher offers pushback, the coach attempts to address it with mixed results. • The coach attempts to use wait time in order to allow for teacher processing, with mixed results.	• The coach uses precise and direct language AND relevant data, OR compelling rationale in order to instill urgency in the teacher. • The coach uses a confident and assertive tone. • If the teacher offers pushback, the coach addresses it. • The coach uses wait time in order to allow for teacher processing.	**In addition to the criteria listed in the proficiency column,** • The coach uses precise and direct language, compelling rationale, AND relevant data in order to instill urgency in the teacher. • The coach's consistent use of direct language leads to an observably efficient use of time whereby additional time is created for application and reflection.
Questioning	• Few or no questions are asked which affects the investment of the novice teacher in the conversation. • Open-ended questions are not used. • The coach asks several leading questions which affects the teacher's participation in the debrief. • Most of the conversation is dominated by the coach which leads to a lack of teacher processing and engagement.	• The coach attempts to use questioning to invest the novice teacher in the conversation, though does not employ a variety of strategies. • Open-ended questions are present but at times are not strategic (overly scripted). • The coach asks some leading questions rather than questioning for the sake of seeking understanding. • Parts of the conversation are dominated by the coach which leads to limited teacher processing and engagement.	• The coach uses a variety of questioning strategies to invest the novice teacher in the conversation. • Open-ended questions are strategic (to involve data, to allow reflection, to uncover mindsets, to encourage participation of novice teacher in the development of action steps) • The coach strategically uses questions to seek to understand. • The conversation is balanced and leans more towards focused teacher processing and engagement.	**In addition to the criteria listed in the proficiency column,** • The coach uses a variety of questioning strategies to <u>get at the core driver of teacher and/or student behavior</u> (why the behavior is happening). • The coach moves away from scripted questions because the level of engagement and genuine curiosity lead to customized reflection on the part of the teacher.
Student Achievement Data Integration	• The coach misses an opportunity to introduce student achievement data based on key lever.	*• There is evidence which demonstrates the coach has planned a general approach to discussing data with the teacher* *• There is a missed opportunity to collaboratively analyze student data to inform action planning or the data analysis is driven entirely by the coach* *• There is no evidence of a data-centered goal for the teacher's classroom*	*• There is evidence which demonstrates the coach has specifically planned with the teacher's developmental and/or student achievement data context in mind* *• Coach and teacher collaboratively analyze student data to inform action planning* *• There is evidence of a data-centered goal for the teacher's classroom that is referenced as part of the debrief or as an element of follow-up.*	**In addition to the criteria listed in the proficiency column** *• There is evidence which demonstrates the coach has consistently and strategically planned with the teacher's developmental and student achievement data context in mind in order to target strategic and specific gaps.* *• Coach and teacher collaboratively analyze class and individual student level performance or sub-population performance* *• There is evidence of a data-centered goal for the teacher's classroom that is referenced and used set benchmarks and progress monitor towards the goal*

Commitments	
Continue doing…	Start doing…
•	•

2

CHAPTER 2 **Building Teacher Relationships**

First and foremost, you must create relationships through which collaboration, transformation, and innovation can occur.

The education of students is an incredibly powerful and incredibly exhausting experience, especially for someone at the beginning of their career in the field. With that being said, teachers must feel as though they are supported as people, as well as professionals, in order to be their best in the classroom. As we work for and alongside our novice teachers, we must seek to ensure that as many interactions we have with them support them as individuals and develop them as educators.

Every meaningful interaction must start with an authentic connection based on empathy and identity.

Recall once again your thoughts and feelings during your first days in the classroom. Hopeful? Tentative? Invigorated? Terrified? All of those at once and more?

The outset of a journey finds someone at their most optimistic and vulnerable self. One unthinking comment can crush a dream, and one heartfelt, sincere suggestion can inspire a career. The gulf between the two can be razor thin. The teachers in your care are transparently, if awkwardly, exposing their efforts to your scrutiny. If you truly join them on a journey beyond competence to excellence, sharing and experiencing their successes and failures, and becoming their champion, everyone will be the winner—you, the teacher, and the students.

In practical terms, the last thing we want is for teachers to feel nervous or to fear that they are being judged. For most people, it can be difficult to separate what they do from who they are. Novice artists encounter this duality when their work is critiqued. In fact, many hopeful artists of all stripes have retreated from the creative life because they failed to overcome the tendency to take a critique of their work as a personal attack. If a teacher tenses up every time he is observed, or feels that feedback is an attack, it can actually prevent his growth and may encourage him to leave the profession entirely.

Like anyone else putting themselves on the line, teachers need to feel safe. They need to feel heard and seen. They must be able to trust you, because you will be observing them in the classroom at all levels of refinement. They must believe that your goal is not to create a robot that follows the rules of a program, but instead is to nourish their strengths, helping them become the most effective teachers they can be in the service of the students and student achievement.

First Steps

The rest of this book provides the mechanics of affecting that transformation. The point of this chapter is to guide you in creating that all-important connection without which nothing will be accomplished, while at the same time laying out the map that will guide you both on the journey.

Building transformative relationships with teachers is so critical to effective coaching that it is one of the foundational domains of our coaching rubric.

	Building Transformative Relationships		
NOT MEETING EXPECTATIONS	APPROACHING PROFICIENCY	PROFICIENT	MASTERY
The coach does not employ active listening strategies.	The coach sometimes employs active listening strategies (adopting teacher language, paraphrasing teacher's thoughts, think time before responding) with mixed success.	The coach employs active listening strategies (adopting teacher language, paraphrasing teacher's thoughts, think time before responding) in order to better understand the teacher's perspective and increase teacher investment in the conversation.	In addition to the criteria listed in the proficiency column, • The teacher engages in conversation in a way that indicates buy-in (adds in own ideas, tweaks suggestions to fit specific classroom and student context) • The teacher recognizes his or her own strengths and/or focus areas and as a result is motivated to collaborate around implementation of feedback. • There is evidence that the novice teacher has implemented prior action steps.
Mutual respect and trust are not evident.	Mutual respect and trust are evident in the interactions between the coach and novice teacher at times (tone, body language, vulnerability, risk taking, honest exchange). At other times, the novice teacher may demonstrate a lack of respect for and/or a trust for the coach or the coach may demonstrate a lack of respect for and/or trust of the teacher.	Mutual respect and trust are consistently evident in the interactions between the coach and novice teacher (tone, body language, vulnerability, risk taking, honest exchange).	

Building Transformative Relationships			
NOT MEETING EXPECTATIONS	APPROACHING PROFICIENCY	PROFICIENT	MASTERY
The teacher's current personal and professional circumstances are not addressed or considered.	The teacher's current personal and professional circumstances are addressed but not considered when developing action steps.	The coach has or is developing a broad context for the teacher's current personal and professional circumstances, and that context is considered when developing action steps.	
The coach does not identify the novice teacher's strengths.	The coach identifies the novice teacher's strengths, though connections between these strengths and focus areas are not always made clear.	The coach recognizes and reinforces the novice teacher's strengths and uses these strengths as leverage points to impact focus areas (transfer).	

Read through the language of the proficient on the rubric domain for building relationships. Coaching conversations that are positive and productive contain these elements; however, there is no magic formula for achieving this. The strategies discussed below are meant to increase the likelihood that you will be able to engage in effective coaching conversations with a wide range of teachers early in the school year.

Establish a Connection

The first step of building a relationship is to get to know your teacher. Since you may work with a dozen or more educators, sitting down with each for an hour or two before the school year begins is probably impractical. One alternative is to initially gather this information through a survey or questionnaire. You can mitigate the impersonal nature of this step by preemptively providing your own answers so they can see that you are willing to open up, encouraging them to do the same. The advantage of this approach is that it allows your teachers to process the questions at their convenience and provide a considered response, increasing the value of the information. Keep in mind that the survey doesn't replace the initial coaching conversation, but it makes it more effective by allowing you to connect more quickly during the meeting.

In addition to any information you are personally interested in learning about your teachers, this questionnaire could allow you to discover:

Demographics. Family background, hometown, education, and other personal details give you insight into the individual and suggest points of connection. Make special note of their birthday, which can be a powerful point of connection if recognized and celebrated.

Motivations. Educators come to teaching for a variety of reasons that can include a love of the content area, positive experiences as a student, a joy in leading others to greater knowledge, and other passions. Knowing what brought a teacher to the classroom gives you insight into what motivates them and reveals ways that you can support them in the classroom.

Some teachers may be highly motivated by helping their students achieve high scores on exams. Others may value the overall improvement made by some students. Others still may value imparting a deeper knowledge of the content to students and connecting it to a real-world issue. Knowing the aspects of student achievement that motivate a teacher will help you engage them.

Pro-Tip: Teachers will share some motivations with you explicitly. Others will be discovered through the course of the relationship. All of them are worth tucking away to utilize at an opportune time, such as when a teacher feels discouraged. Have a private, central location, either physical or digital, where you can record this information as it comes up, and use this document when sitting down to plan a coaching conversation.

Interests. Interests are as varied as the individuals that pursue them. Be it sports, music, theater, art, family, cuisine, or any other pursuit, you can build an ongoing relationship by sharing in their passions. It's often helpful to ask, "Who are the important people in your life?" Knowing the names of people close to your teachers and following up throughout the year by asking about them lets your teachers know that you care about the person behind the professional.

Strengths. We all have strengths, even if we might be unaware of some of them. One teacher may have a high level of content expertise or a love of learning new things. Another may have highly developed organizational skills or the ability to connect with students individually. Another may have an especially captivating presence in the classroom. Discovering strengths is especially helpful for novice teachers who transition to teaching from other careers. Knowing what comes naturally to a teacher will help you establish a starting point for building competence in other areas.

Values. Values reach to the core of the person. Knowing the personal values of your teachers will not only give you insight into what drives them, but will also allow you to take measures to honor them as you coach them. For example, if a teacher strongly values family, ask questions about individual family members at the beginning of a debrief, and prioritize their time with their family when giving them action items.

Working style. Does the teacher work through things offline or talk through issues? Start with the big picture and work down to the details or the reverse? The Myers-Briggs Type Indicator (MBTI) is one commonly used method for gaining insight into the personality and working style of an individual and can give you ideas about how to approach debrief sessions. If you don't have the capacity to engage with programs like this, simply asking people to self-report on their working styles will give you insight into what they value and how they approach their work life.

Set Expectations

At the outset, you must establish the nature of the coaching process and the relationship so that the teacher knows what to expect. As you play more roles in a novice teacher's life (coach, evaluator, principal, etc.), this process becomes simultaneously more complicated and more necessary. At Teaching Excellence, we set expectations through an Initial Coaching Conversation. For most of our teachers, this is done during our onboarding sessions at your new teacher induction. For teachers who are hired after these sessions, the coach should initiate this conversation with each teacher individually sometime in the first two weeks of coaching. In that conversation, we cover:

Touchpoints. The primary interaction will be through a series of "touchpoints," which is what we call our coaching interactions. These range from classroom observation and debriefing to analysis of student achievement and teacher performance. See the chapters on "Observing in the Classroom," "Flow of a Debrief," and "Alternate Touchpoints" for more information.

Communication. Be sure the teacher knows that you will be sending them emails and calendar requests to schedule meetings, and that they must be responsive in acknowledging them promptly. It's a good idea to establish a timeframe for responding to emails and phone calls, usually within 24 to 48 hours. If your campus or district has specific expectations for timeliness and style of communication, make sure you explain those at the beginning of the year. Helping teachers avoid the confusion that can come with a new set of communication norms will pay off for both of you in the long run.

Norms. When setting expectations, let the teacher know the importance of starting and ending meetings on time, sharing openly, and staying focused during coaching conversations instead of attempting to multitask by grading papers or answering emails. Emphasize the necessity of communicating a scheduling conflict as soon as it arises, as conflicts often crop up during the school year. When these norms are established from the outset, it is easier to hold teachers accountable to them when they do not follow through.

Feedback. Let the teacher know that the coaching process begins with the first observation and debrief. You both will be hitting the ground running, as the calendar of a school year waits for no one. Reinforce this sense of urgency during each debrief. Also tell teachers why feedback is important, and start to build their mindsets around growth. Let them know that you are here because you care about their success and the success of their students. Remind them that all your feedback is given to reach common goals.

Transparency. Advise the teacher that most of what transpires in the coaching relationship affects others on your campus (and potentially across the organization) and will be shared with other stakeholders. Reiterate that you'll share both their strengths and areas for growth with other stakeholders to ensure aligned support. It's better for them if everyone who observes their classroom and supports them is on the same page.

Confidentiality. The coach-teacher relationship involves a personal level of communication and trust. Assure the teacher that anything shared in confidence will remain between the two of you, unless it violates the law, of course. For example, if a teacher needs advice about how to handle a difficult conversation with someone else on campus, you will hold that coaching conversation in confidence. If you support multiple campuses as a teacher educator, highlight the distinction between your role and that of the evaluator, assuring them that if they need to confide in you about a potentially sensitive issue, such as a problem with a colleague or supervisor, meetings are a safe space. If you work on a single campus and are the teacher's evaluator, assure them that issues shared in confidence do not impact their instructional evaluations.

On the Journey

Once the year picks up, the schedule settles into episodic engagements and interactions. Here are some techniques and suggestions on how to maintain and deepen your relationship with your teachers:

Observations

During an observation, your goal is to be a presence, not a participant. Remember, a presence can project a mood—one that has the power to intimidate or calm. Before you reach your teacher's classroom, you must establish a mindset that determines the type of presence you will project during the observation.

When you observe, it's important that you keep a neutral to positive face relative to what's going on in the classroom. If things are generally smooth in terms of student behavior, then a little smile is good. However, if the classroom is chaotic, the students are disruptive and the teacher looks frazzled, a smile wouldn't be appropriate, but neither would an expression of disapproval.

Sit in an area of the room where you won't draw attention to yourself. Ideally, business as usual should continue in the classroom while you're there so that you can get an authentic picture of life in that classroom and your support can be as targeted as possible. You can also sit with students when your focus areas are more instructional and you're curious about their work, but make sure that they can't see what you're writing or typing about the classroom. When you find it desirable to circulate through the room, it is best to do so when students are working, rather than when they are in the middle of more teacher-led activities.

Debriefs

Chapter 7, "Flow of a Debrief," covers the elements of this interaction in detail. Here we focus on the opportunities within the debrief session to establish and build the teacher relationship.

Build in get-to-know-you moments

When we're on the job, and even off campus for a meal or an event, it's easy to fall into the routine of talking about work. However, in reality we don't live such compartmentalized lives. What happens at home can affect our work, and vice versa. Consequently, it's important to create a structure that puts the person before the professional.

That's why the first part of each debrief is set aside for catching up on what's going on at home. As you get to know your teachers, the conversation should move beyond the generic "How was your weekend?" or "How is the week going?" to asking about what you know is going on in their life. Has there been a marriage or a new baby or a move? Perhaps a sports tournament or concert or theatrical performance? By caring about the things that matter to them, you show that you care about their lives outside of the classroom.

In addition to building a connection, it's important to have some idea of what is happening in their non-work life because it can influence how you approach the debrief and the feedback you will provide. Is there something that might increase or decrease their motivation or drive? Something that might nudge them toward a defensive reaction when receiving critical feedback?

In the classroom, we call each other by our "teacher names" (i.e., Mr., Ms., Mrs. ____). One way of moving from the professional to the personal is to use their first name at the beginning of a debrief when talking about their non-work life, saying "Tell me about how Stephen is. We'll have plenty of time to talk about Mr. Ruiz in a moment."

The structure of an effective debrief should also account for time to discuss the positive elements of a teacher's classroom and practice (we call these "glows"). Even if a teacher is struggling mightily, they need to know what is going well because this helps them replicate that success. It also helps reinforce their trust in you as a coach—someone who will always help them see the positives in addition to the areas for improvement. Celebrate their progress and point out times they have implemented your feedback to positive effect. Ask them what they think they are doing well, so that they pay just as much attention to their "glows" as their "grows" and continue doing what makes them successful rather than throwing the baby out with the bathwater as they work to improve other areas of their instruction.

Engage in active listening

Glance around the room in a restaurant at all the people together but individually engrossed in their smartphones, and you'll have to agree that we live in the most distracted age in history. When someone takes time to truly listen, people notice. Active listening involves certain techniques that increase the quality of communication and give the speaker the assurance that they have been heard and understood.

It begins with body language—specifically displaying an open posture. Face the teacher directly without crossed arms or legs. Make eye contact and nod to indicate you understand. Wait until the teacher is completely finished speaking before responding. When you do respond, it can help to adopt the language style of the teacher. For example, if they use sports metaphors, such as "I thought I hit it out of the park" or "I really fumbled the ball on that one," mirror that when appropriate. Paraphrase what they have said to verify that you do understand their point, even if you don't agree with it. When you ask questions, be patient and comfortable with silence as the teacher takes processing time before responding.

Monitor air time

In a coaching situation, it can be tempting to launch into a monologue, especially if your observation has uncovered a major issue that needs to be resolved. But the teacher must be an active participant in the process, as they will be the one who does, or does not, implement what you discuss. Build in questions that prompt the teacher to process the feedback, internalize it, and mitigate potential obstacles. For example, after sharing a glow, ask, "What have you been doing that resulted in students beginning their morning work right at the bell in your classroom?" At the end of a debrief, prompt the teacher to share their take-aways from the meeting rather than restating the action steps. This not only gives them a chance to process and potentially clarify your expectations going forward, but reveals to you which messages and information stuck.

Build trust through respect and vulnerability

Trust is the foundation of the coach-teacher relationship. The teacher must consider you as reliable as a conductor's watch. There should be no doubt that when you make a commitment, it is as good as done. If you say you're going to observe a particular class period, you are there.

In addition, they will trust you when they realize that you respect their opinion and their confidentiality. Conduct debriefs in a place that offers a suitable level of privacy. Ask before sharing sensitive information with other stakeholders. Ask for their thoughts on the feedback you provide to them and which classes to observe next. Honor their time by planning feedback on a manageable number of key levers that the teacher will need to accomplish for an upcoming lesson.

When you share struggles you have experienced in your own career, you humanize yourself and give the teacher hope that they can win through in their own struggles. You can even share current challenges you are facing and how you're working to conquer them. As the English writer G.K. Chesterton said, "The point of fairy tales is not to warn us of the danger of dragons but to show that dragons can be defeated."

Build on strengths

Recognize and reinforce the teacher's strengths and use these as leverage points for growth whenever possible. For example, if a teacher plans engaging and meaningful content connections into the openings of their lessons, point out that this strength can help with classroom management. They have proven they can successfully implement their content objective—most likely by imagining the thought processes of their students. Explain that this same mentality can be used to help them effectively communicate behavioral expectations within a lesson. When they set behavioral expectations and explain how meeting those expectations will benefit the students in a way that speaks to them, the students will be more likely to comply.

Connect feedback from one debrief to the next. This highlights their progress and builds a sense of continuity for the teacher's professional development, making it more likely that the teacher will sustain the momentum going forward.

Monitor the relationship

Relationships are not a set-and-forget thing. They are dynamic and need attention to thrive.

One conversation about working styles and the coach-teacher relationship at the beginning of the school year isn't enough. During the year, as the cycle of touchpoints progresses, issues will inevitably surface.

Motivations are worth revisiting when a teacher is really struggling. Pulling them out of the weeds and reminding them why they chose this work can be just what a teacher needs to get them back on track.

On the other hand, a teacher might become defensive to feedback or respond to questions in a curt manner. If left unaddressed, this rift could damage the relationship to the point of threatening student achievement and teacher retention. Trust your intuition and name instances when this occurs so that you both can process them and move forward together.

At times, you may work with a teacher who lacks humility and isn't willing to admit to his or her faults. For example, this type of teacher might say that the strategy you suggested is something he/she does on a regular basis, that he must have forgotten to implement it during your observation. It is also necessary call out this inconsistency using data from the observation, such as the number of students on task or the percent of students who correctly answered questions on an assignment, to address this pushback. As trust is built, we have found that the overwhelming majority of teachers begin to open up, acknowledge their faults, and truly desire the feedback of their coach when feedback is consistently given in this manner.

Periodically, you must perform a temperature check on the relationship, monitor its vital statistics in the form of a discussion prompted by questions such as:

- What about this relationship is working for you?
- What isn't working?
- Do you think our communication is effective?
- What do you need more of?
- If something needs to change, what change would you prefer?

Based on the discussion, establish commitments for change on either or both sides and identify a time for the next temperature check. At Teaching Excellence, we do this formally four times a year, and while your calendar may differ, we would recommend discussing a similar list of questions at least twice a year with the teachers you support.

Reinforce the Connection

Make time to connect with teachers outside of the routine meetings, such as at a campus-wide or system-wide professional development day. An activity that requires extra effort for the teacher, such as an event, a service project, a field trip, or a special lesson that requires extra preparation or room set up, are excellent opportunities for what our coaches have nicknamed "Whatever It Takes Time." These are the periodic moments when you have the time in your work to provide extra assistance for your teachers to help them get a leg up. While these "Whatever it Takes Times" may only occur a few times in a given school year, every connection you make with your teachers builds the foundation for an effective teaching career that could ultimately change hundreds or thousands of lives. And isn't that why we're all here?

Relationships are not only the foundation of the development of masterful teachers, but of successful educational communities. These same principles can be used to improve the quality of all professional relationships (and personal, for that matter—though that is beyond the scope of this book). When novice teachers are surrounded by these strong relationships, we have found that they feel as though they can be their true selves in their classroom, which allows them to be better educators faster.

~ CHAPTER REFLECTION ~

1. Recall a productive working relationship you've had with a mentor, manager, or senior colleague. What were some initial actions that person took to help establish a relationship of mutual trust and respect?

2. When you conclude debriefing with a teacher, how do you know they were bought in to the feedback you provided? What actions, words, tone, etc. do you look for? What did you do during a debrief (where buy-in was high) that contributed to the teacher's motivation to implement the feedback?

3. Temperature-check the relationship of a teacher you support. What questions do you need to ask to see how they feel about your working relationship and the support they're receiving?

3

CHAPTER 3 **Building Stakeholder Relationships**

While the relationship between the teacher educator and the teacher is important, there are other people with both a stake in the outcome and opportunities to drive the development of the teacher. Your combined efforts will be most effective if all the stakeholders work together to guide the novice teacher toward excellence in the classroom and in the teaching profession.

The Power of Partners

The first year in the classroom can be challenging enough on its own. If the teacher is flooded with an abundance of conflicting advice, it can be confusing and discouraging. Consequently, it is hard to overstate the importance of a strong partnership between the teacher educator and the other stakeholders.

The stakeholders you will engage, and their titles, will vary depending on your organization's environment. These may include:

- Campus administrator (assistant principal, principal)
- Evaluator or instructional support such as a Dean of Instruction or academic evaluator
- Special education teachers and support professionals
- District content support
- Dean of students, campus culture leader
- Grade-level chairs or new teacher mentor
- Certification program stakeholders
- Program supervisors, such as a college of education, Teach For America, The New Teacher Project, or similar teacher and leader development organization

There are two ways to ensure that teachers are not overwhelmed by feedback. Stakeholders should agree both on the current performance of the teacher, normed feedback, and on the correct course of action, aligned feedback.

Normed	Aligned
everyone agrees on how things stand	everyone agrees on a course of action
what is now	what is next

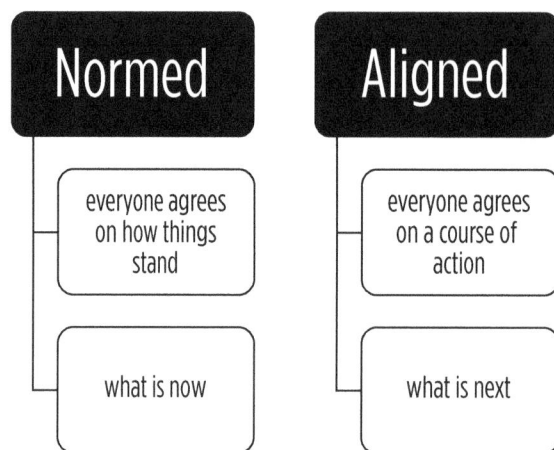

As the teacher educator, you must take the initiative to assure that all stakeholders are normed and aligned. At the outset, all stakeholders need to have a similar understanding of the abilities of the teachers you will be coaching and the challenges they must conquer. The concept of a strong first-year teacher might mean different things to different people. There may be varying views regarding to what degree a teacher is struggling or flourishing, or which issues should be prioritized.

As the team converges on the course of action for a teacher's development, you must make sure that all stakeholders are aware of who will take ownership of each action. For example, a teacher may need to improve on presentation of new material. The coach could focus on an instructional strategy to check for understanding, while the evaluator could guide the teacher on meeting lesson plan deadlines and using district resources to create lesson plans. If you serve as both the teacher educator and primary evaluator, you may collaborate with a mentor teacher or grade level chair to provide this dovetailed support. Focus areas should usually be complementary rather than identical, and never conflicting.

Pro Tip: If a teacher is struggling significantly, it may be helpful to have one or two defined focus areas with clear criteria for each. Each person who observes and/or plans with the teacher should reference the criteria in his/her feedback to the teacher and copy that feedback to all other people involved so progress and struggles can be noted.

This expectation can create anxiety in some teacher educators, particularly those who feel ill-suited for building a network of relationships. If that is you, relax. Success in building impactful stakeholder relationships is not dependent on a personality type. It is dependent on implementing a concrete set of skills and strategies that can be taught, learned, and implemented regardless of personality type. The key to success is adopting a growth mindset, the same thing you hope to instill in your teachers. All that is required is that you believe stakeholders' alignment is important and devote time and energy to the steps covered in this chapter. This is not a trick or technique you pull out when issues crop up. It is something that must be maintained throughout the year for the benefit of the teacher and their students.

First Steps

You should prepare for your first meeting as you would prepare for an important job interview. If you are a coach who serves multiple campuses, research the campus until you can tell its story. What is the history of the campus? What grade levels does it support? What is its mascot? Does it have a focus such as STEM or world languages? What is the cultural context of the school or surrounding community?

If you are coordinating stakeholders at your home campus, reflect on past collaborations with those stakeholders. What was a situation in which the collaborative efforts produced the most ideal outcome? Where is there room for improved or streamlined support for novice teachers? What current systems might need to be adjusted to make collaboration more efficient or effective?

You can get some of that from online research, but dig deeper. Seek out other teacher educators who have supported teachers on the campus to get a more personal and in-depth understanding of the environment, including what has worked in the past and what might need to be tweaked.

First Meeting

Your first meeting should include all the stakeholders connected with the roster of novice teachers you are supporting for that campus. A combined meeting of all the stakeholders for a campus may happen only a few times a year. Depending on the number of teachers you are supporting, the meeting should be scheduled from half an hour (a few teachers) up to an hour (five or more teachers).

The first order of business is to continue your information-gathering phase.

Begin with the big picture. What is this year's vision for students and teachers? Are there any campus initiatives regarding academics or culture or other areas of focus? What campus-based professional development efforts are planned that will affect teachers and their growth trajectory? If you are a teacher educator at a single campus, you may have already had a vision-setting meeting with the administrative team. Regardless, it is still critical to think through how campus initiatives will involve and affect the novice teachers specifically. For example, you may have a campus-wide initiative to incorporate literacy across all subjects. You must account for the level of support a novice teacher will need while participating in the initiative. Should the evaluator and the campus literacy specialist co-observe? If a teacher is struggling with both behavior management and instruction, who will support each respective area of development?

Then bring it down to the focus of this meeting. What is their view of an ideal partnership? Which teachers on campus are candidates for a classroom observation with one of your teachers? Who is considered a stakeholder for each teacher you will support? How much capacity does each of these individuals have for observing and meeting with teachers? If you are not housed on this campus, where is the

41

best space to hold meetings and debriefs? Where is the best place to work when privacy is not required?

Finally, get down to logistics. Be sure to get access to the schedules of the stakeholders. Get a consensus on how often the stakeholders should meet and the touchpoints to keep in sync between meetings. Identify the stakeholders who should be kept in the loop for specific issues, including planning and instruction, classroom culture, and professionalism.

You also need to discuss the protocol of coordinating feedback from multiple sources. When one stakeholder provides feedback to the teacher or teacher educator, which other stakeholders should be informed? How will the feedback be communicated? For example, if you provide feedback on how a teacher is implementing IEP accommodations in their lessons, you might copy the Special Education team leader. Or, if you provide feedback on a teacher on an improvement plan, you may copy the teacher's evaluator, supervisor or school leader.

If circumstances prevent a deadline or action step from occurring on a deadline, how will this be communicated to the pertinent stakeholders? When should other stakeholders be copied on an email to a teacher?

Establishing these kinds of details up front prevents the dreaded "oh-by-the-way" moment, where someone who should have been in the loop suddenly discovers that things have changed.

Once you have mined other stakeholders for information, share your vision of coaching and the trajectory of professional development you have in mind for your teachers. Finish by confirming the strengths, areas of focus, and action items each stakeholder has committed to. End by thanking them for their participation and their contributions.

Check-Ins

As your coaching progresses, you will want to have regular check-ins with any stakeholders who regularly work directly with your teachers. While you may have a set of concerns and a course of action in mind, come to the meeting with a collaborative spirit. Some stakeholders may have an agenda of their own, informed by their independent interaction with the teacher and their own professional expertise and personal viewpoint. As with teacher debriefs, every meeting should begin with a few minutes of personal connection.

Primary stakeholder first check-in

Regardless of whether you are a campus administrator, grade-level chair, or instructional coach, you will meet one-on-one with primary stakeholders frequently depending on how many teachers you share with the other person. As an instructional coach, you will check in with administrators and evaluators who also support your teachers. As a grade-level chair or content leader, you may check in with both instructional coaches or administrators who support teachers on your team. Consider the roles in your district or context, and who you should collaborate with regularly to best support teachers. For each stakeholder, you should devote some time at the beginning of your first individual meeting to gain insight into the person you will be working with. This takes the panoramic view of the campus you acquired at the first meeting and drills down to the individual. What brought them to education in general and their current role? Their favorite aspect of the profession? If they have participated in collaborations before, find out what worked well and what didn't. What does this stakeholder look for in a collaborative partner?

Then get down to practicalities. What is their preferred means of communication? Which platform is optimum for sharing feedback on observations? Once these details are settled, you can get down to the focus of this and all other meetings.

Regular check-ins

During regular check-ins, first cover the status of novice teachers who require attention, such as a struggling teacher. A teacher progressing satisfactorily (whose progress you have communicated with the stakeholder through other channels such as email) may not need to be discussed.

For the relevant teachers, share the glows and grows (see Chapter 7, "Flow of a Debrief") you've tracked from your observations, starting with the teachers who seem to be struggling. Move on to professional development events scheduled for the campus with a view to how you can help to increase the effectiveness for each of your teachers.

Conclude with a review of action steps and schedule the next check-in.

If a stakeholder discusses a situation regarding a teacher without providing action steps, follow up immediately. You could ask, "The next time you go observe Andrea in the classroom, what do you want to see?" Or say, "Just so I'm clear, I am going to coach on planning and delivering the teacher model, and you are going to . . ." Push them into stating a clear action step.

There may be times in these check-ins when you discover that your views of how a teacher is performing or the best course of action are not aligned. In this situation, share data that backs up your viewpoint and ask for data about the other viewpoint. Work with your stakeholder to figure out the root cause of what you are seeing in the classroom. There may be times that you defer to the other person's priorities, especially when that person is formally evaluating the teacher.

Campus administrator

If a teacher has a coach who does not serve in an evaluative or administrative role on the campus, then the relationship between their coach and their evaluator is very important. Within a week or two of your group stakeholder meeting, these two parties should schedule an individual session to work out the details of the process going forward. After an initial get-to-know-you session, the first order of business is to establish the frequency of future meetings. To assure continuity, it's best to set a standing meeting time that is held sacred on your calendars. Then agree on the protocol of each meeting, the level of preparation required to assure an efficient and efficacious meeting, who will populate the agenda (one or both), and the processing style of the participants.

Depending on personality type, some people prefer to solidify their thoughts ahead of time while others prefer to engage in discussion to arrive at a solution. The point of this step is not to pick one style for the meetings, but to allow everyone to honor the processing style of all participants.

It is beneficial to revisit the strengths and focus area of all the stakeholders so that the teachers grow from this shared expertise and experience.

Next Steps

As the school year progresses, you will need to devote attention to maintaining the relationship with your teachers and stakeholders for your teachers. A little forethought can make the process feel natural and effortless and will authentically deepen the connection.

Campus

When working on campus, choose a workspace that is visible to administrators and teachers. This practice increases the perception of your presence as a common and natural event, and encourages spontaneous conversations. If working at several campuses, learn and use campus-specific terminology including acronyms and the term used for the students, such as "scholars" or "KIPPsters."

Extend the "Whatever It Takes" practice you adopt for your teachers to the campus. When possible, attend selected campus events—dances, field trips, sporting events, and the like. YES Prep has a regular practice of gathering volunteers from the home office staff to assist teachers with the reading and grading of open-ended-response questions on district wide common assessments. Offer support on testing days as a floater or hallway monitor. Attend campus professional development sessions and use the focus of these sessions when providing feedback. Maybe even collaborate on or host a campus PD event if you have an area of expertise that is aligned to a campus initiative or focus area.

Stakeholders

When you encounter another stakeholder of one of your teachers, whether casually or in a scheduled meeting, reinforce the connection by asking about something personal to them that they have mentioned before.

Keep individual stakeholders in the loop via their preferred communication method by sharing glows you observed regarding a teacher you both support. Ask for input or recommendations on a growth area. Ask them to co-observe or co-debrief when appropriate. And always hold sacred and thoroughly prepare for every check-in.

Teachers

In addition to the intense relationship building you're already engaged in with each teacher, look for opportunities to incorporate feedback from stakeholders. For example, "Great job implementing the feedback from the Literacy Specialist when you were presenting the new vocabulary words. Because you provided visual examples that were clear, students were able to remember the words when they encountered them in the text." This type of purposeful statement allows the teacher to see that they have a united team supporting them that is aligned on a common message, reinforcing the validity and substance of the message. When possible, attend a check-in between the stakeholder and the teacher. If the teacher has a strained relationship with the stakeholder, this might create tension in your relationship with the teacher. They may get the impression that you are siding with the stakeholder instead of advocating for them. To avoid that issue you could ask the teacher about their relationship with the stakeholder and clarify the benefits of the group meeting.

Wrap Up: Staying on Course

While regularly maintaining these relationships will be a continual practice, our work cannot be done in siloes. Just like with your teachers, it's a valuable practice to occasionally check the temperature of the relationship with other stakeholders. Invite feedback about what is working and not working and what they would like to change, if anything. Commit to follow up on any suggestions and schedule a check-in to follow up.

Once you have established the foundation for a connected network of strong relationships among an entire team of teachers and stakeholders, you will find everyone's efforts are maximized.

~ CHAPTER REFLECTION ~

1. Who are the other stakeholders in your teacher's development? List their names and positions.

2. When have you been most successful in your collaboration with these individuals? What were some missed opportunities to support teachers more collaboratively?

3. Think of a teacher that you currently support. Where in that teacher's support or development is there an opportunity for you to collaborate with another stakeholder?

4

CHAPTER 4 **Organizational Skills**

"Organizing is what you do before you do something, so that when you do it, it is not all mixed up" — A.A. Milne

If we are to fully maximize the impact of this connected network of stakeholders to improve teacher performance and student achievement, then we must acknowledge that time is one of our most precious resources. Because of this, the first skill-based tools a teacher educator needs are primarily organizational. Teacher educators must be incredibly well-organized and live from their calendars, which are planned days in advance so that every minute can be used purposefully to help novice teachers grow. However, the struggle to remain organized and on course must not take precedence over the relationship between you and the teacher. Amid the apparent chaos, it is important to be flexible, equitable, and strategic while engaging your teachers with a spirit of generosity. Otherwise, the relationship can suffer from either a lack of responsiveness by the coach or a lack of time management by the teacher. A poor coaching relationship can affect teacher effectiveness, student achievement, and teacher retention.

Planning a schedule for all the interactions with your teachers can sometimes feel like trying to predict the shape of a cloud an hour from now. Teacher educators have to be even more organized with their schedules than other school or district staff so that they can balance the needs of many different teachers and classrooms. An unexpected field trip or an impromptu meeting scheduled by another administrator can ripple through a schedule like falling dominoes. This can be equally problematic for campus-based coaches such as deans or principals, whose competing interests constantly fight for priority. While this might cause you to question the value of spending time maintaining a calendar, the reality is that only a high degree of organization supported by a carefully planned and well-maintained schedule will allow you to recover from the unexpected and achieve the goal of being flexible, equitable, and strategic.

There is an anonymously written story circulating the web about a teacher (sometimes also billed as a professor) who makes a powerful analogy for their students in class one day. In this story, the teacher takes a jar, places a stack of large rocks inside and asks the students whether the jar is full. After some discussion, the teacher then fills the remainder of the space with sand. In some versions of story the teacher continues with pebbles and then water, but the ending message is the same: The jar represents the time you have available to devote to various endeavors, both big and important, and smaller, more tedious ones. The teacher reminds their students that, if you fill the jar first with all the small business, there is little room left for the big important items. Thus, when you fill a jar with rocks and sand, you must put the rocks in first. The analogy is relevant to our time management priorities as teacher educators: When you create your personal schedule, you must schedule the most important things first.

Teacher educators can rely on school bell schedules to structure both observations and meetings, but may need to hold longer blocks of time to complete other responsibilities. Being intentional about calendaring ensures you will be able to accomplish all your goals.

Schedule Goals: The Rocks

In a typical six-week grading cycle, a bi-weekly interaction allows you have at least three touchpoints with a teacher. For the sake of continuity and momentum, it's best not to go longer than two weeks between sessions with most novice teachers. In addition, a struggling teacher might require more frequent interaction. The extra meetings may not require a full-length 50-minute debrief, but they should still provide focused feedback to reinforce consistency in implementing the skill under development. For an experienced, highly effective teacher, a three-week cycle might be appropriate. Regardless of the level of the teacher, schedule your debrief to occur within 48 hours of the observation so that the memory of classroom events is fresh in the respective minds of you and your teacher.

Pro-Tip: It is important to familiarize yourself with the expectations and calendar of the campus so that you don't schedule an interaction that conflicts with a standing meeting or special event. For a district-based teacher educator, this might involve asking to be added to campus email lists or gathering PD calendars well in advance. A campus-based teacher educator should make note of all campus activities that may affect the staff members they coach so that they do not accidentally double-book their teachers.

Pro-Tip: Schedule the debrief before the observation. The debrief is generally more challenging to schedule due to limited planning periods and other duties the teacher may have during this time. Conversely, it is much easier to find time to observe the teacher. We recommend meeting during a teacher's planning periods rather than outside of the school day. Schedule meetings before or after school only as a last resort.

Administrative Tasks: The Sand

In addition to the tips outlined above, consider the following:

- Schedule time to plan the debrief. The length of time will vary depending on your level of experience and whether the content of the debrief is routine or challenging. For example, you may be able to quickly jot down notes for a focus area on which you frequently coach. On the other hand, even an experienced coach may need to schedule additional time to plan a conversation about a particularly challenging situation, or a conversation with a teacher who might not be receptive to the feedback.
- Schedule time for lunch. This might sound trivial, but when things get hectic or behind schedule, some coaches may be tempted to skip lunch. Don't make that rookie mistake. Instructional coaching is a demanding profession, and you have to be working at the top of your game—not running on fumes—for your last debrief of the day.

Other tasks that must have a time slot on your calendar include:

- Email (teachers, colleagues, and other school stakeholders)
- Business details (filing, tracking, certification requirements)
- Professional development (internalizing and writing sessions for campus staff, or specific group of teachers)
- Check-ins with other administrators who support your teachers (bi-weekly or as needed)
- Check-ins with your direct manager
- Meetings
- Other tasks for which you are responsible (teaching periods, campus duties, deadlines, etc.)

If something must be done and it takes more than a few minutes, put it on the calendar. We recommend that you have no gap larger than 30 minutes in your schedule. If you have several things to do that will only take five or ten minutes, schedule a block labeled "Work Time" and record the task list in the description.

Making the Most of the Time

No schedule is immune to change. Here are a few tips for making the best use of your time and your teacher's time.

- As you plan a block of time on a campus, consider some fallback options that allow you to accomplish secondary goals at that location during that time.
  - If a meeting falls through: Do a few impromptu check-ins on other teachers, depending on their availability. This could include quick observations with brief written feedback rather than conversations.
  - Look for a "Whatever It Takes" opportunity with another teacher. (See Building Teacher Relationships.)
  - Use the time to catch up on housekeeping items.
- If several teachers are struggling with the same issue (e.g., time management, lesson planning, teaching from multiple rooms), plan a

breakout session for the group instead of working with each teacher individually. You can follow up individually by scheduling observations after the session to check on implementation. This will both save you time and connect teachers to other professionals on their campus who are focused on the same set of skills.

Being Equitable with Time

Teacher educators have the same goal for all their teachers, but those teachers don't all start their journeys from the same point. As you strive to be flexible, equitable, and strategic, you may find that you are spending more facetime with teachers who are struggling than with those who are more advanced.

In this situation, it is important to remember that equitable doesn't mean equal. It means fair and reasonable. To avoid the perception that you are showing partiality to struggling teachers, you could let your advanced teachers know that coaching takes on a different aspect in response to the development level and needs of each teacher. Don't hide the ball from your teachers, let them know that they may see you less often because they are doing well, and that they should still reach out to you between meetings if they need additional support.

Tracking Time

Given the sheer number and breadth of a coach's responsibilities, their calendar is the linchpin of their organization system. Ideally, all participants—teacher educators, support staff, teachers—use the same calendar system, maintain it regularly and share their calendars with all concerned. If you are coaching in multiple districts, you may not be able to share calendars, even if they all use the same platform. If you are a campus-based teacher educator, your team should move towards a unified vision around calendaring as a campus to streamline communications if you don't currently have a system in place.

At Teaching Excellence, everything goes on the calendar (even lunch and driving time between campuses), using a consistent, team-wide naming convention. It's a helpful strategy to have your own unique color-coding system that helps you keep appointments discernible at a glance.

In the interest of being equitable and strategic, create a rough sketch of how many teachers you need to see on each day; it's ideal if you can plan this at the beginning of each six-week period. If you go to multiple campuses, consider which campuses you'll visit and when. You may even be able to identify who you will prioritize and what types of coaching interactions will be most effective. This plan avoids gaps in interactions for any given teacher. As you set weekly goals in the calendar, you can reserve extra slots for teachers who need additional support.

Color Coding and Nomenclature

Color code your appointments by location or activity. For example, all observations and meetings at a particular campus (or if you're at one campus, of a particular subject or grade level) would be the same color. A best practice we've learned over time is not to assign the color for the meeting until the recipient accepts the meeting. This technique allows you to see at a glance what has been accepted and to send a reminder if necessary.

Use consistent abbreviations in the description for common activities and locations. Include the initials of the attendees in the description. Number observations and debriefs to make the level of progress clear at a glance. Naming conventions make tracking your observations much easier.

Common Calendar Items	
Category	Protocol
Walk through observations	OBS_HB or WT_HB (observation of teacher with the initials HB)
Time to prep. Include type of prep (e.g. coaching conversation planner, model lesson)	Work Time or Prep Time – write specific task. — i.e. Prep MG (teacher's initials) coaching conversation or lesson plan feedback for MG
Email	At least one 30-45 minute chunk- recurring appointment per day
Calendaring	30-60 minutes per week
Drive time	Drive, 20-30 minutes minimum
Lunch	Lunch, 30-minute recurring appointment
Meeting, debrief	MTG_TB/TE, DBF_TB/TE TB/TE indicates a teacher with the initials TB and your initials as Teacher Educator
Check-in with other administrators or stakeholders who support this teacher (weekly or every other week)	Check-in_MG/TE Again, the first set of initials represents the other person and the second set represents your initials

By close-of-business on Friday, 80 percent of interactions for Monday, Tuesday and Wednesday of the following week are scheduled in our calendars and invitations are sent. By close-of-business on Tuesday, 100 percent of the week, Monday through Friday, should be finalized. We recommend shying away from scheduling anything with teachers either sooner or later than that timeframe so that you can stay flexible while meeting everyone's needs. Events on our calendar that we do not need to attend (but want to remember when they are happening) remain uncolored and/or tentative to indicate we are not attending. Overlapping appointments are avoided when possible.

Fitting It All In

When you're working with more than a dozen teachers across multiple campuses, or even more teachers at a single campus, creating a schedule that covers everything in a six-week period can be a challenge. Here's one method to make everything fit. For this example, we'll assume a load of 16 teachers across two campuses over the course of one six-week period. The same steps apply for districts that use nine-week quarters or teacher educators that support one campus.

Boundaries and blackout dates

Establish the beginning and ending of the six-week period and block out the following blackout dates:

- First and last day of the six-week period
- District-wide or campus-wide teacher professional development days
- District meetings you are required to attend
- Team building and professional development for teacher educators
- Holidays, including early dismissal days, spring break, other holiday breaks, etc.
- Non-instructional days: district or campus-wide exams, state assessments

Deadlines

In the first week, it's important to schedule time to conduct an initial classroom walkthrough to observe each of your teachers in action. No debrief is required for this observation. The primary value of this exercise is to get a temperature check on your cohort to aid you in strategically planning the first six weeks by prioritizing teachers of greatest concern. You should also schedule two full touchpoints in the first six weeks.

Touchpoints

The last step is to calculate how many touchpoints you have to schedule, how many days you have available, and the resulting number of touchpoints per day (or week) you must schedule to stay on course.

In this example, once we block out the blackout dates (including a half day to account for weekly meetings and check-ins), we end up with 18 days. We have three touchpoints per teacher, multiplied by 16 teachers, for a total of 48 touchpoints. Divide this by 18 days, and we should plan to schedule have three touchpoints per day.

Tracking Communications and Status

You should develop a consistent method for documenting status and interactions with teachers, support staff, and other stakeholders. For each campus, keep a record of each teacher's schedules. It can be as simple as a three-ring binder or folders, but an electronic approach is easier to share and copy. If you are a teacher educator working at multiple campuses, a quick way to start this process is to email the action log and other debrief notes to the teacher after a meeting and copy their campus evaluator (more on this later). If you work on one campus, you could still send this log to your teacher and copy all other collaborating parties to increase transparency. You can create an email folder for each of your teachers to store emails from the evaluator or other stakeholders regarding your teacher. This streamlines access as opposed to sifting through a lengthy inbox for a document.

If you are a campus-based teacher educator, you likely have some system in place for keeping track of a teacher's evaluation performance. Many organizations have a standard software platform that allows teacher educators and campus administrators to record their feedback in a common place. The teacher is able to see all their feedback and action items in a central location.

Tracking Touchpoints

If your school district utilizes a detailed teacher evaluation system, your method for tracking touchpoints can indicate the type of touchpoint and how the teacher is performing. This allows you to strategically plan the next steps based on past observations.

Name	Obs	DB	Obs	DB	Obs	DB	Obs	DB	Duration	Focus (From Rubric)
Teacher A										
Teacher B										
Teacher C										
Teacher D										
Teacher E										
Teacher F										
Teacher G										
Teacher H										

Figure 2: Paper HITs Tracker

And the Rest

We also recommend a folder, either paper or electronic, to store notes or templates from check-ins with your manager, stakeholders, and team meetings. You may also want separate folders for common coaching tools that you use, feedback that you receive, and professional development sessions you give.

Scheduling your time in this way may seem unfamiliar and overly structured, but we have found that clear time management and scheduling protocols help our coaches get the most out of each of their interactions with teachers. When coaches can schedule their time carefully, they can devote more attention to the teacher relationship and individual coaching conversations.

Mastering organizational skills can be the critical element that enables success for a teacher educator. By using our system, which works for professionals who coach teachers at several campuses at a time, you can create time in your schedule for the important tasks of building relationships and providing the feedback and experiences that enable your novice teachers to grow and excel.

1. What are the "big rocks" that you need to prioritize for your scheduling?

2. When, during your day or week, do you sit down to organize your time and workflow for that week? If you do not have this practice established, try to carve out 30-45 minutes at the beginning or end of your week to do this.

3. Who are your teachers who need the most critical support — and therefore the highest number of touchpoints? How long will this intensive support last? Account for this on your personal calendar.

5

CHAPTER 5 **Observing the Classroom**

The next large chunk of this book will center around those actions that many immediately think of when they envision developing teachers. By this, we mean the act of sitting in a classroom to gather data to inform your coaching interactions with the teacher with the goal of increasing the student achievement in that classroom. The standard interaction between a teacher and teacher educator in the Teaching Excellence program takes place when the coach observes the classroom, takes time to independently process what they saw at both the teacher and student level, and clearly communicates this information back to the teacher. From here, the coach can help a teacher build skills and develop strategies that will ultimately result in positive change in student achievement. Because such a large percentage of our interactions follow this "observation-debrief" format, we have devoted several chapters to detailing each step. This chapter will focus on the time that the teacher educator spends observing a classroom. Effectively observing a classroom involves preparation; this allows you to make the most out of your time in the classroom and maximizes the effectiveness of the following debrief.

Before You Walk In

When you're making professional phone calls, one best practice is to smile before you pick up the phone. The startling reality is that even though the person on the other end can't see your expression, they can hear it. Your expression affects your vocal inflection, regardless of your mood before dialing the phone.

In the same way, it's important to prepare yourself, both mentally and emotionally, before you turn the knob of a classroom door and enter.

Establishing an Objective

Every observation should be planned with a manageable set of goals based on the developmental level of the teacher. For example, early in the year your goal would be to diagnose the teacher's level of development in classroom management and instruction. On a subsequent observation, your goal would be to see how feedback from the previous debrief is implemented. The goal of an observation following a lesson-planning debrief is to evaluate the effectiveness of the lesson the teacher planned. Teachers will progress gradually through tiers of development like the ones captured on the TE Rubric; you will need to consider the teacher's current tier and whether they are ready to move on to more complex skills or whether they need other skills within the same tier. If a teacher has concerns about one or more students or a specific class, you would go into the observation with the goal of discovering the details and forming a plan to support the teacher.

Initial observation

YES Prep instructional coaches conduct an initial management walkthrough for all teachers enrolled in the Teaching Excellence program within the first ten days of classroom instruction. While this step assures compliance with certification requirements from the state of Texas, we have also found it to be a best practice regardless of physical location or mandated observation requirements. The data gathered during the observation is used to diagnose the teacher's developmental trajectory and classroom effectiveness in the domains of instruction and classroom management. If your school or district has an established rubric for evaluations, you should couch this diagnostic in the language of that rubric, though it does not need to simulate exactly this evaluative process.

For example, consider an evaluative rubric that has a domain for instruction and five instructional indicators for content knowledge, communicating new information to students, student practice, differentiation, and anticipating student misunderstandings. When evaluating a novice teacher at the beginning of the school year, it is less critical to diagnose their ability to differentiate instruction or anticipate student misunderstandings. Using the language of your rubric, you would focus your diagnosis on the appropriateness of the content, the clarity with which the information is presented, and the level of student engagement.

At YES Prep, our TE instructional coaches use the TE Rubric, which is tiered version of the district's Instructional Excellence Rubric (IER), modified to prioritize items relevant to the developmental trajectory of a first-year teacher.

While all areas of the rubric are relevant, focus primarily on classroom management and student engagement during the first observation. Specifically, take note of how the teacher promotes a positive climate, establishes routines and procedures, and develops a sense of urgency. If the teacher confidently gives directions in a calm and authoritative manner, they are well on their way to building a positive rapport with students. On the other hand, if the teacher seems tentative and intimidated, or uses harsh language or an aggressive tone, the first lever to pursue will involve classroom management.

Maintaining continuity

There are several sources you can draw on for determining the most relevant objectives of an observation session. After the first observation, you will have diagnosed the teacher's current level of effectiveness with respect to your instructional rubric. By reviewing the next level up, you can easily get a broad sense of the objectives for the debrief and the next observation. If you find a teacher has a considerable need for improvement in multiple areas, coordinate efforts with the relevant stakeholders to divide and conquer. If an online tracking system is available, use it to further research the trajectory of the teacher and any feedback left from previous interactions with additional stakeholders.

From these various sources, you can determine the focus/key lever and then create the substance of your debrief session (see Flow of a Debrief) including the glows and grows (see Glows and Grows) and action steps, which will narrow the focus of your goals for subsequent observations.

For each debrief, as the year progresses, you should review the action steps the teacher agreed to from previous sessions. The coming observation will result in either a glow or a grow, depending on how well the teacher is implementing the action steps. For example, you might say, "I noticed you implemented the feedback we discussed and practiced last time. You clearly stated your expectations for practice and used positive behavior narration to point out which students were doing this correctly. As a result, three of the 25 students corrected their actions, and you created a warm environment in your classroom. Excellent job."

Sometimes the teacher or another stakeholder will ask you to observe a specific aspect of the class, perhaps something the teacher is struggling with or a new skill that they are implementing.

Establishing a duration

While a class may last for 45 or 50 minutes, you should stay for the full session only if the goals of the observation require it. For example, some districts or states require a set amount of time be spent in a classroom observing during an evaluation. In some cases, the action steps for a teacher may involve the full trajectory of a class, or the transition from instruction to group practice to individual practice, and so a longer observation is required.

On the other hand, if the skill under observation is establishing a "Do First" element to transition the students from entering the room to getting settled and on task, the observation might be 15 or 20 minutes. Some coaches opt to stay in the classroom for the full period and prepare the coaching conversation. Regardless of the duration, while you're observing, you should be free from distraction and focused on what is happening in the classroom.

One of our instructional coaches had an experience as a novice teacher in a traditional public school with a primary evaluator who was also the principal and carried a walkie-talkie to stay in touch with other staff.

"Even though she would turn the volume down on the walkie-talkie when observing, it was obvious that her attention was split between my classroom and solving issues over the radio, frequently stepping out of the room to respond to messages. I became disheartened. I would have understood if she had to leave to deal with an emergency, but it seemed as if my classroom and my development as a teacher was taking a backseat to the business of running a campus. If she slated time to observe my class, she should have set aside the minutiae of the daily routine for 20 minutes to focus on the observation. I felt less valued and, subsequently, less trusting of her as a stakeholder in my development."

Advance Notice

Most observations are unannounced. You want to engage the teacher and the classroom as it normally functions, not observe a group prepared to be on their best behavior. However, there are occasions where advance notice is desired or required.

For a debrief where you and the teacher prepare a lesson plan together (see Chapter 12), obviously the teacher will know when the observation will occur. For an action step related to lesson design and facilitation, you may want to review the lesson plan and reference it during the class. In that case, you may need to contact the teacher ahead of time to get a copy of the lesson plan.

Pro-Tip: Access the teacher's lesson plan to peruse as you observe the classroom, usually after you've collected student data and other notes. Teachers may have to print lesson plans or may upload them to a common website. You can also ask for the teacher's lesson plans in advance.

In the Room

You serve as a second set of adult eyes in the classroom. Teachers make hundreds of tiny decisions a day, and part of your role is to help them see those decisions. Your goal is to capture as much relevant data as possible to establish a basis for the teacher to buy into the lever and areas of focus you will discuss in the debrief.

Capturing Notes

You should settle on a platform for taking notes ahead of time. Whatever method you use, it must allow for the quick recording of multiple elements of a dynamic environment. Many teacher educators prefer running notes.

Running notes use a two-column layout to show the teacher's action and the student action, providing a source for evidence-impact statements you can use during the debrief, such as, "When you did [action], the students [reaction]." This cause-effect relationship can be substantiated with quantitative data, such as the number of students showing mastery in practice or the number of students correctly following the steps.

Depending on a coach's personality type, the information might be based on an intuitive reading of the room. For example, the coach may perceive that students know what to do but are choosing not to get started for some other reason. Use that impression to guide you in collecting additional data. For example, follow up by asking some students what they are supposed to be doing or count the number of students who are off task.

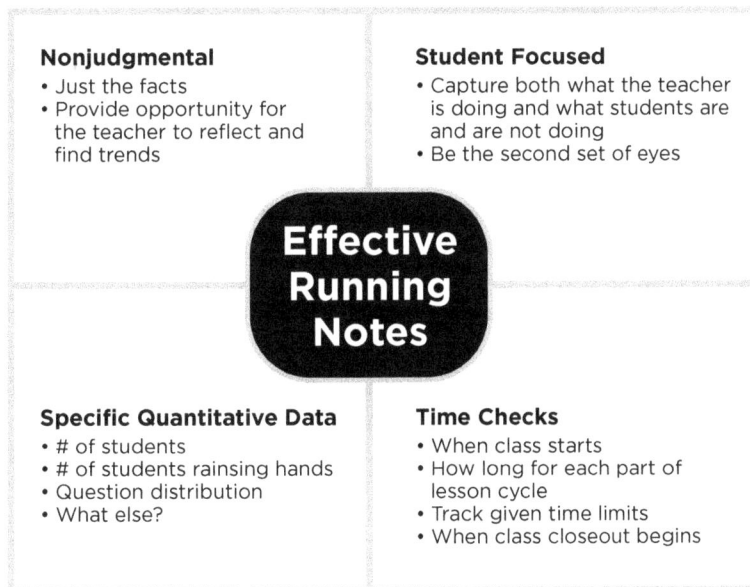

Nonjudgmental
- Just the facts
- Provide opportunity for the teacher to reflect and find trends

Student Focused
- Capture both what the teacher is doing and what students are and are not doing
- Be the second set of eyes

Effective Running Notes

Specific Quantitative Data
- # of students
- # of students rainsing hands
- Question distribution
- What else?

Time Checks
- When class starts
- How long for each part of lesson cycle
- Track given time limits
- When class closeout begins

In your coaching, it's critical to remember that while the changes you want to see in the classroom are often changes in the students (improvements in academics or behavior), the agent of those changes will be the teacher. When in the classroom, look for teacher actions and the subsequent student outcomes.

Teacher Actions	Student Outcomes

• What checks for understanding does the teacher ask and do the students answer correctly?
• What type of feedback does the teacher give to students during or after student practice?
• What does the teacher say (or not say) that causes students to move/act/perform in an effective way?
• What does the teacher refer to or model which sets students up for success (or not)?
• What scaffolds or supports is the teacher making available (or not) which students need to be successful?
• What is the ratio of teacher talk vs. time when students have a chance to think, write, read, and speak?
• How urgent does the classroom feel? How urgent is student action? What teacher actions are contributing to or hindering this?
	• Behavioral and Cultural
	  – The number of students on task after the teacher states an expectation
	  – The way students and the teacher speak to and interact with each other
	  – How students follow routines and procedures
	• Academic
	  – How closely student work resembles the teacher model
	  – The accuracy of what student produce verbally, in thought and in writing
	  – The number of students given the opportunity to process the material

Sometimes you will immediately recognize an area that is clearly a strength or something that needs improvement. In this case, take the time to go beyond noting the incident to capture enough data to prepare constructive and affirming feedback for the debrief or for a glow and grow note you can leave at the end of the observation. This practice increases teacher investment, providing the teacher with an increasing awareness of the moments when they are effective, marginally effective, or ineffective.

Capturing Student Data

Student data can provide the evidence necessary to convince the teacher that a gap exists or to show a teacher how the gap manifests itself in the classroom. Data can reveal trends in student work, highlight student understanding and misunderstanding, and illuminate root causes of issues in the classroom. How to integrate student data into the coaching conversation is discussed in detail in later chapters.

Rule number one in any conversation is to know the audience. Before collecting data, you should know who is in the room. Not just the teacher, but the students as well. For example, try to determine the ability levels of the students relevant to the task at hand. If you observe a history lesson that involves reading a primary source document, it's helpful to know whether the document is at the appropriate reading-ability range for students in the class. To determine the suitability of the document, you must know something about the average reading level of kids in the room.

The more you observe a group of students, the more you will be able to reference (and plan for) their personalities and ability levels. A coach will also gain this knowledge over time by asking the teacher clarifying questions during debriefs about specific students.

In 50 minutes of a class session, you can experience hundreds, if not thousands, of impressions. It takes practice to develop a filter to select the relevant information that will build teacher competence. We categorize student data into three types—observational data, student outcome data, and student achievement data. The types of data are presented in the following table, along with examples of each.

Observational Data (quantitative data not linked to student work)	Student Outcome Data (completion of student work)	Student Achievement Data (quality of student work)
*"It took **12 minutes** for students to enter the classroom and complete the 'Do First.'"*	*"When the timer went off, 80 percent of students had completed the 'Do First.'"*	***"Nineteen out of 25 students success-fully completed** the first problem they attempted after the teacher model."*
*"After **each key point**, students had a chance to **process in two ways:** through written reflection and then sharing with a partner."*	***"Out of the ten problems** students were supposed to complete during guided practice, **five out of six groups only got through problem four."***	*"Within the two groups I observed, **four of the ten students** wrote a thorough response to the short answer question that included **two or more vocabulary words."***
*"You issued a conse-quence to **three of the five students** that called out an answer (rather than raised their hands)."*	*"After the first turn-and-talk, **three sets of partners** did not record an answer to the question."*	***"Two out of five groups** incorrectly answered the 2nd guided practice problem by choosing **letter B instead of letter C."***

While all types of data are useful, the most important is student achievement data because it provides evidence of student mastery of the material, which the primary goal of instruction. It may be difficult to collect student achievement data at the beginning of the year due to a focus on management and classroom culture. If, as the year progresses, it seems student achievement data is still unavailable (because the introduction of new material runs long, students did not have the opportunity for independent practice, etc.), this is data in and of itself that must be addressed in the debrief.

It is best to capture impressions with your instrument of choice as they occur. However, there are a few key observations that need attention.

A question. When the teacher poses a verbal question to the class, make note of which students respond and what their responses are, verbatim. Did the teacher follow up appropriately to an incorrect or incomplete response, or did they fill in the right information and move on? Knowing this information will can help you identify a key lever, and can also help deepen the teacher's understanding of how their students are internalizing the material. For example, "I recorded that all of the 23 students answered the question on their guided notes. However, only 12 of 23 answered correctly. The most common incorrect answer was _____."

A time limit. When the teacher gives a specific time limit, record the result at the deadline. For example, if the teacher tells students they have two minutes to solve a problem independently, note the starting time, the announced duration, the actual duration allowed, and the number of students who completed the exercise. A novice teacher will frequently allow too much or too little time as opposed to the announced time.

Collecting examples of student work. If students turn something in during class, and you know the teacher isn't going to grade them immediately, borrow the work to analyze before your debrief.

Pictures of student work. Ask the students if they mind (they usually don't) and start capturing pictures of their worksheet, paragraph, or whatever it is they're working on. This works well for both group and independent work.

Videos of student work. If students are working on a more complex task or something that involves a lot of movement, such as a lab investigation in science or an exercise circuit in a PE class, shooting a quick one- to three-minute video might be useful. Videos are also great ways of capturing student discussions during small group or partnered discussions.

Student interviews. On some occasions, interviewing students in the classroom can provide context and helpful feedback to guide your debrief planning. The questions should be simple and allow for direct answers. For example, you might ask, "What are you learning today? Can you tell me why this topic is important? How does it connect to what you learned earlier this week?"

Interviewing students can provide insight into a focus area for teacher growth. For example, you might ask, "I noticed you wrote ____ on your paper. Can you tell me why? Did your teacher walk you through the steps to answering this question? Where can you find those steps?"

Tally marks. These are great for keeping track of student behavioral data, such as compliance on tasks, number of students participating, or number of teacher warnings/redirections/consequences given. You can get really fancy with this one and create a ratio of warnings to consequences. Tally marks can also be used for student achievement data, such as the number of correct responses in a given time.

Time. It's important to take note of how long certain tasks take or how much time is spent dedicated to specific events.

- Behavioral: How long does it take to complete routines, such as entering class, cleaning up after an activity, transitioning from one activity to the next?
- Academic: How much time is spent on direct instruction compared to student practice? How long did the PowerPoint last? How long did students watch the video before it was paused and they were given an opportunity to process or take notes?

Audio. In some cases, it may be helpful to capture audio recordings of a teacher in action. One instance where this is particularly helpful is when you are coaching a world-language teacher or a bilingual teacher and the goal is to increase the amount of time spent speaking in the target language to the class. Audio can also be helpful when coaching a teacher on authoritative voice. Volume, intonation, rate of speech, and side chatter can all be noted.

Individual student data. When available, previous student performance data can useful.

- The number and type of questions the teacher asks to low, mid, and high students
- Which students volunteer
- Which students immediately engage in a task
- Which students are most and least engaged
- Which students are partnered with each other and the success of the partnerships

Capturing student data is useful because it:

- Helps you determine cause-effect relationships between instruction and student outcomes
- Informs your selection of the key lever
- Creates teacher buy-in and urgency around implementing new skills

In addition, you can collaborate with the teacher in analysis to determine trends, guiding the teacher in methods of looking at student outcomes to inform course corrections going forward.

Typically your presence in the classroom should be as unobtrusive as you can make it while gathering the information you need to engage the teacher during the debrief. It's a situation not unlike birdwatching. You stand in the field or the woods and wait, becoming part of the environment until the birds dismiss you as a threat and go back to their normal behavior. Students and the teacher need to get used to your presence as an observer, not a participant. The sooner you become invisible, the sooner you will begin to get the most honest view possible of the classroom.

A campus administrator may have a lower threshold and be more likely to intervene due to their established presence on a campus as a figure of authority. In the case of a teacher educator, there is usually no need for intervention if students are off-task or misbehaving slightly. However, a situation may arise that prompts you to intervene. Pushing, hitting, threatening, bullying language, objects flying across the room, anything that causes one or more students to feel unsafe, emotionally or physically would be grounds for intervention.

Before you intervene, ask yourself two questions:

- Is the teacher unaware of the situation or is not addressing it?
- Would a parent be seriously concerned if they saw this being said or done to their child?

If the answer to either of these questions is "yes," then intervene. Otherwise, save it for the debrief.

On Your Way Out

It is common practice for Teaching Excellence coaches to leave quick written feedback, either in note form or as an email, at the end of the observation, especially if the debrief isn't until the next day. For written feedback, both the glow and grow should be something easy to communicate and quick to implement. Save more complex feedback for the debrief. The glow should be positive feedback that had a demonstrable or substantial impact on student learning. In the note, you can shout out a practice that went well, a student who is improving, or something that's different in a teacher's lesson that's going particularly well. The grow left on a note should a quick correction the teacher could do immediately upon reading your feedback. For example, if you notice a major issue with the way the teacher is explaining key points, but see a more minor issue with student behavior, you would address the student behavior in your note and leave the clarity of instruction for your debrief. You might tell the teacher to make sure they face students when presenting material, rather than turning their entire body toward the board.

Pro-Tip: If you leave a grow in a handwritten note immediately after an observation, put it where the teacher can see it but not the students. The teacher's areas for improvement don't need to be made transparent to students. For example, if the teacher's desk is very cluttered, maybe leave it face down on their computer keyboard. Use fun pens or stickers to add some joy factor to a glow left behind in a note. Teachers are then more likely to keep them, reference them, and it helps to build the relationship and create a positive association with feedback. Also, take a photo of the glow to file in the teacher's folder for tracking and accountability.

teaching excellence	
Walkthrough Feedback	
Teacher: Andrea Rivera	Date: September 8
Way to GLOW...	**Way to GROW...**
During INM you consistently held students accountable to raising their hands and not calling out answers. It helped that you proactively stated this expectation before posing questions. As a result you reduced the number of off-task conversations and disruptive comments.	Twice you called on the first student to raise their hand. You can increase participation by providing the entire class with "thinking time" before calling on specific students to answer. I.e. "after I project the question, I'm going to give everyone 30 seconds to read it and think of answer. Raise your hands when the timer sounds." Adding the wait-time increases the likelihood that everyone is engaging with the question.

After You Leave

The observation is act one. It sets the stage for the debrief. In the hours after the observation, you must mold the multifarious data you have collected into a compelling case for change. (See Identifying a Key Lever.)

While you will coalesce a multitude of impressions into a course of action, everything you advocate must be based on data. Regardless of the strength of your impressions, if the data do not support the key lever you have identified, you might not have the proper key lever for this teacher and this classroom at this moment.

While data can be used to create buy-in and investment on the part of the teacher, you can also use it to create goals with which to measure improvement behaviorally and academically. For example, you might note that during the observation, after the teacher posed a question, only three students out of 18 raised their hands to answer. After suggesting strategies to increase student participation, you can invite the teacher to set a target for participation for the next lesson and follow up on this target during your next observation. Or a teacher poses a question to the class, but none of the students who respond use academic vocabulary specific to that lesson. If you coach on increasing students' use of academic language, you can measure the improvement in frequency across observations by collecting this type of data.

You should be aware of common pitfalls associated with sharing data. Too much data can overwhelm the teacher and become a source of discouragement rather than progress. Also be wary of cherry-picking data to prove a point. Take care to verify that the data you have collected represents a variety of students at all levels of achievement.

A live classroom has many moving parts, and the presence of an observer has the potential to be disruptive. With a clear focus, careful planning, and thoughtful engagement, you can minimize the potential for disruption and maximize the effectiveness of an observation. This allows the teacher educator to gather accurate data, which will then ensure that the next steps in this observation-debrief process will have the maximum impact on teacher growth.

~ CHAPTER REFLECTION ~

1. What is your relationship to the students in the classrooms you observe? Do they significantly adjust their behavior when you walk into the room, or are they accustomed to your presence as an observer?

2. Before you go into your next observation, reflect on the following.

   a. Where is this teacher in their developmental trajectory?

   b. What type of student data are you looking for (observational, outcome, achievement)?

   c. What will you do to gather this data such that it can be integrated into your debrief?

4. Using a varied approach to data collection can provide you with a holistic perspective on a classroom. What is a data-collection strategy you haven't flexed in a while? What is an upcoming opportunity to do this in practice?

6

CHAPTER 6 **Identifying a Key Lever**

"Give me a place to stand, and a lever long enough, and I will move the whole world." — Archimedes

When you walk out of a novice teacher's classroom from an observation, you have likely seen several things that, if changed, would make the classroom better. However, just as you would never present all nine parts of speech or all 39 trigonometric identities in a single class session, so must you resist the urge to catalog all the areas for improvement in the debrief following the observation.

For feedback to be actionable, it must be targeted and developmentally appropriate. If a teacher is struggling with classroom management, you will have to hold off on feedback about lesson pacing and transitions until the class is in a place to benefit from that growth. Generally, as with everything, you start with your rubric. Identify which of the focus areas is the most foundational, and begin there. In fact, it would be a good idea to have a copy of your rubric handy as you read this chapter.

Understanding Levers

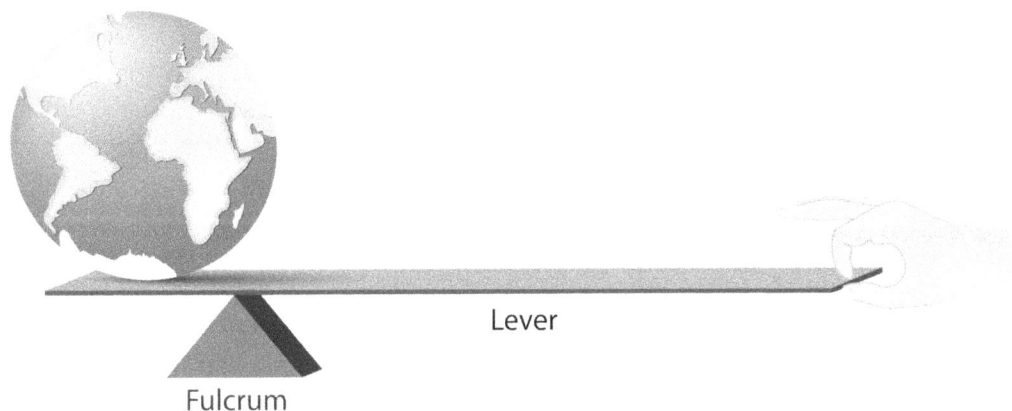

A lever is a force multiplier, the classic example of working smarter. The lever and the fulcrum work together to magnify the power of an individual. The closer the fulcrum is to the thing to be moved, the less effort required to move it.

To align this metaphor to Teaching Excellence, you first observe the classroom and then identify an area for growth drawn from the rubric. You would then refine the action you want the teacher to take in order to improve. In this process, you ask yourself: What's the single change this teacher could make that would most significantly impact students? The closer that action is to the developmental level of the teacher, the greater the power of the action step.

A key lever is an instructional practice identified for the improvement of classroom management and/or instruction that can significantly improve student achievement. It is the highest priority feedback to deliver in a debrief. It should not be tied to a specific lesson or content area. Instead, it should advance a pedagogic principle or classroom management strategy that can be applied in a variety of classroom situations.

For example, if a math teacher's explanation of how to convert percentages to fractions or decimals is confusing, the key lever is not advice on a better way to explain that process. The key lever is advice regarding best practices on how to explain content. Even that broad area needs to be specified into a single action, like how to execute an effective teacher-model of any skill, concept, or process, breaking down a concept into student-friendly steps, using visuals, and thinking through how students will follow along during instruction. Keep in mind that the debrief may use the specific observed lesson as an anchor to illustrate how to apply the skill – this will be covered in Chapter 11: Application and Practice. Selecting a generalizable key lever ensures that the teacher walks away with a replicable skill that is applicable to any relevant future lessons, rather than simply gaining a good trick for teaching one specific lesson.

A key lever is	A key lever is not
• Aligned to a rubric • Developmentally appropriate • Narrow in scope • Skill-based • Transferable to many lessons • Targeted to student performance	• An entire section of the rubric • Action steps alone • Applicable to only a single lesson

Based on a Rubric

For feedback to be effective, it must have a context. Otherwise debrief sessions can descend into nothing more than a random list of tips for things to do in the classroom. That is why a rubric is an essential element of the process. A rubric focuses your vision on how the teacher should be functioning in the classroom at the end of the year.

By using a rubric, you can address foundational skills first, and then incrementally build on that foundation. The process creates an environment of iterative progress—growth, mastery, growth, mastery—allowing the teacher to look back with a sense of achievement at each step. The encouraging power of this practice cannot be overstated and is a major tool in building competence and confidence.

Take care to isolate a key lever that addresses the root of the issue rather than a symptom. For example, if a teacher is struggling to manage the classroom and is yelling at students, you may want to explain that it is important not to yell. However, the root issue is not the yelling, it is that they need to develop the skill to state clear expectations and follow through consistently. You'll be able to provide them additional feedback on things like tone of voice during the application portion of the debrief. Common root issues to look for include:

- Will vs skill – coach needs to determine if the teacher doesn't agree with the feedback around management tactics, or they are simply missing the mark on implementation?
- Lack of "with-it-ness": Is the teacher generally unaware of misbehavior occurring?
- Fear of students' reactions to redirections or consequences
- Wanting to be friends with students rather than an authority figure
- Lack of authoritative voice
- Teacher wants to push through misbehaviors and focus solely on content

Once you have a key lever, create a list of three to five explicit criteria for success to use in the debrief that will empower the teacher to consistently replicate this skill and create action steps for applying these skills in upcoming classes until the teacher has mastered them. See Chapter 8, "Criteria for Success" for more information.

Developmentally Appropriate

TE created the trajectory of a novice teacher based on more than a decade of organizational experience in training thousands of people new to the field of teaching. This experience shows that even teachers with strong content expertise have capacity for greater student achievement when they first establish a strong culture and demonstrate proficiency with classroom management skills. For this reason, the TE trajectory prioritizes these skills alongside the foundational components of pedagogical training. This approach contrasts with traditional university education programs, which may offer a single course on management but emphasize educational theory and curriculum.

The trajectory of a novice teacher is based on average teacher performance. A coach should always respond to the actual, observed needs of the classroom. If someone is demonstrating proficiency in one of the earlier skills, you should feel empowered to move forward with higher-level skills. Be careful, though, that these proficient skills remain firm throughout the school year.

During the first two or three weeks of the school year, coaches should prioritize support around setting clear and high expectations for student behavior and consistently holding students accountable to those expectations. Then move on to establishing and maintaining effective routines and procedures throughout the class period. Questions you'll ask about routines may include:

- How should students enter and exit the classroom? What will the first and last five minutes of class look like?
- How are materials distributed and managed?
- How should the teacher get the attention of the whole class?

By the end of the first six weeks of school, a novice teacher ideally should be demonstrating proficiency in these skills and the basics of lesson planning. If a teacher is still struggling with these foundational skills, resist the temptation to move forward. If students aren't consistently listening to the teacher and are non-compliant, more complex teacher skills like questioning strategies and differentiation will still fall flat because the students aren't engaged. Rather than continue along the path of the traditional observation-debrief cycle, consider the strategic use of alternate touchpoints for a new approach to building skills around classroom management. See Chapter 11 on alternate touchpoints for more information. In this instance, you might:

- Demonstrate the skill in a model lesson
- Co-observe an accomplished teacher with the novice teacher
- Have a direct conversation with the novice teacher about why they are struggling

Once the teacher has achieved proficiency in these Tier 1 skills, shift your coaching focus to Tier 2. This usually happens by the beginning or middle of the second six weeks of school. Tier 2 still places some emphasis on management—maintaining positive classroom culture, maintaining a sense of urgency during instruction, and ensuring that students are respectful towards one another during academic exchanges. Tier 2 begins with a greater emphasis on academic instruction—using visuals to assist learning, breaking complex material into clear ideas, modeling the skill, and ensuring that students have ample opportunity to process the information and demonstrate their learning.

Grounded in Student Data

Using data moves the conversation from the subjective to the objective, allowing you to demonstrate to the teacher the need for change and the impact this change can produce in their classroom, both behavioral and academic. This can take the form of quantitative data, such as the number of students showing mastery in practice or the number of students correctly following the steps, and qualitative data, such as the level of achievement during individual practice. As you reflect, ask yourself:

- What was the teacher teaching?
- What were students producing as a result?

- What was the quality level of instruction? (alignment, modeling, checking for understanding, questioning)
- What was the quality level of student achievement? (following criteria for success, independent practice work, exit ticket/quiz/test data)

Your campus or district may have a particular focus, such as bringing struggling students up to their grade-level in skills like literacy or math. You may need to find a way to attach that focus to your feedback. If a teacher is struggling with a more foundational element such as lesson planning, address that focus area first and look for a sustainable developmental track to join up with the campus focus.

Identifying Levers

Identifying the proper lever for focus is a learned skill. It's tempting to latch onto the most obvious item for improvement, but it is important that you take the time to call upon all your experience, skill, and intuition to drill down to the lever at the proper developmental level that will have the most impact. Draw on your own teaching experience and reflect on what you would have done in place of what you saw. The process described below can help you refine your key lever.

How to identify the key lever	
Process	**Questions to ask yourself**
Observe the teacher's actions and subsequent student actions	What are the students doing or not doing as a result of the teacher's planning and execution?
Note gut reactions	What stands out as needing to change? What does this teacher need to start/stop doing immediately?
Reference the tiers	What is the most appropriate root cause for the teacher's state of development?
Check your key lever against the criteria for success	Is the key lever too narrow or too groad? Is it skill-based and transferable? How will this key lever impact student performance?

Observation

As Sherlock Holmes said, "It is a capital mistake to theorize before one has data." Observe, then deduce. (See the chapter on observing the classroom for more information.) When you're observing the classroom, take notes on glows and grows. Gather student data to support throughout the class period. Ask yourself questions to help you limit the scope of your analysis:

- What are the students doing or not doing because of the teacher's planning and execution?
- Based on these notes, is there a common thread that can hit all the things you noted?
- What is the single most important focus from the rubric that will have the greatest impact on the teacher's development and student achievement?
- If I could change only one thing, what is the one thing that could address most of the issues I'm seeing?

Take your time and stay in the classroom long enough to be certain you have identified the right lever. Choosing a key lever too early might cause you to miss clues to a more foundational issue.

Instinct

The human brain is excellent at recognizing patterns, though much of this processing occurs subconsciously. You may find yourself with a gut feeling about what needs to change before you can determine exactly what caused you to feel that way. Memories of your own professional experience—lessons you've taught, classes you've struggled with, professional development you've attended—are stored in your long-term memory and can form a kind of pattern-recognition algorithm resulting in an "Ah-ha! I've seen this before" moment. This is one reason why classroom experience is an important element of a teacher educator. Remain open to these impressions and note them as you sense them. If any part of what happens in the class surprises you, or if you have an emotional reaction, the stimulus is a likely starting point for ferreting out a key lever. Review your rubric to see if your impressions resonate with a foundational skill. Ask questions:

- I am confused. Why?
- What stands out as in need of change?
- What does this teacher need to start or stop immediately?
- Which moment struck me as off-kilter?

Once you have identified a key lever, refer to the rubric to assure that it is appropriate for the teacher's level of development. Look at the supporting levels to verify that the teacher has mastered all the skills required to make this the most powerful agent of change in their development. You might find that a different foundational skill must be mastered before moving to this key lever.

Finally, test the key lever for scope and application. Ensure that the key lever will meet the teacher at their current level of skill, and push them appropriately. Ask yourself: Is it too narrow or too broad? Is it based on content or skill? Is it transferable to other contexts? What specific desired student outcome will be enabled if the teacher acts on this key lever?

Potential pitfalls in choosing a key lever include:

- Choosing the symptom and not the root cause
- Choosing the obvious rather than the most important (pacing vs. transitions)
- Choosing more advanced key levers before indicators in lower tiers are proficient
- Choosing a key lever based on personal bias

Pro-Tip: Consider the teacher's ideal self—their aspiration—and merge that with best practices. During planning, review previous feedback to make sure that the lever aligns with the arc of development and does not conflict with it.

Choosing Between Multiple Key Levers

After the observation, you may be debating several key levers. Rank them by priority and urgency based on the developmental levels of your rubric. If you don't have that system in place, then rank them in terms of foundational skills (need to haves). You'll need to use your intuition to then determine a single focus for the debrief. For example, if a teacher is having a small issue with classroom management (early in development) and has a large issue with student practice (later in development), use what you know about the teacher personally to choose one key lever over another. This exercise should help you narrow down the list to one or two key levers. You may be able to address one area quickly in the debrief, or through a written glow and grow, and save the other for more significant discussion and application. However, when you identify the key lever, remember that it is important to keep the conversation focused on a manageable amount of change for the teacher.

The concept of continuous improvement is based on making incremental but significant changes in an iterative process: changes that build on those made before to accelerate growth, much like compounding interest in a savings account. Establishing the right key lever for each touchpoint helps to keep the novice teacher on track for continuously improving throughout the academic year and their career.

1. Is your current teacher-evaluation system tiered? If not, which teacher-actions will you prioritize for your novice teachers early in the school year? Where would you like them to be in their development by mid-year? By the end of the year?

2. Our program prioritizes proficiency in classroom culture and management before diving deep into instructional development—but you can't start coaching on instruction too late in the year. If a teacher continues to struggle with classroom culture, what is your threshold for transitioning them into instructional key levers?

3. Connecting with other stakeholders can help you identify key levers when supporting teachers outside of your content expertise. Who is a colleague that you could co-observe a teacher with to provide you this perspective?

7

CHAPTER 7 · Flow of a Debrief

You walked into the observation with a purpose. While in the classroom, you identified a key lever and possibly left a quick glow and grow via a written note or an email to the teacher. You also collected data that gave you a snapshot of how students are doing in that class. See Chapter 5, "Observing the Classroom," and Chapter 6, "Identifying a Key Lever," to review these steps.

Now it's time to plan the debrief conversation with the teacher. Everything you've done up to now, relationship building moments, conversations with stakeholders, observations in the classroom, and student data, establishes a context that is critical in your planning.

Good planning before a coaching conversation is evident in the structure and focus of that conversation. Here are the coaching moves that we look for:

Structure/ Focus			
The structure of the meeting is consistently unclear, and the structure of the meeting lacks critical components.	The structure of the meeting is at times unclear and/or is lacking necessary components.	The meeting has a clear and purposeful structure and includes all necessary components.	In addition to the criteria listed in the proficiency column: • The meeting has a clear outcome and the coach incorporates teacher input in referring to that outcome regularly. • The coach significantly modifies the structure of the meeting to address the specific needs of the teacher.
The outcome of the meeting is unclear.	The outcome of the meeting is not explicitly stated.	The outcome of the meeting is explicitly stated.	
The meeting often loses focus on the outcome (conversation includes multiple tangents).	The meeting sometimes loses focus on the outcome (conversation includes tangents).	The meeting remains focused on the outcome.	
Language from the TE Rubric is not referenced.	The specific language of the TE Rubric is rarely referenced during the meeting.	The specific language of the rubric is referenced throughout the meeting.	
The meeting lacks pacing to the point that the outcome is not achieved.	The meeting at times lacks pacing (i.e., too many focus areas, some parts of the conversation are not fully developed, focus area is low impact, too much or too little time spent on any one part of the meeting) which minimizes the impact on teacher action and student outcomes.	The meeting is paced in such a way that the right amount of material pertaining to the outcome is covered, in order to impact teacher action and student outcomes.	

You can work your way through your plan by asking yourself key questions to clarify your thoughts and establish a clear direction forward. The Coaching Conversation Planner (CCP) can help you process what you observed and gather your impressions and thoughts. The Debrief Agenda can help you structure the flow of the debrief. (See the Appendix for these planning tools.) In this chapter, we'll introduce you to the hallmarks of an effective debrief meeting that motivates the teacher to improve their practice.

Purpose and Outcomes

A debrief is a carefully planned and structured conversation between you and the teacher. During the debrief the teacher gains insight into their strengths (glows) and key areas for improvement (grows) as captured during the associated observation, engages in practice with real-time feedback, and has the opportunity to apply the feedback in an upcoming lesson or lesson plan.

Teaching Excellence allocates the bulk of the debrief for practice and application because history has proven that knowledge alone doesn't translate into classroom effectiveness. We have found that teachers who get feedback about how to improve but don't practice it immediately are much less likely to implement the feedback in the classroom. Modeling a skill and providing structured practice contributes to teacher effectiveness and success in the classroom.

Because debriefs are typically executed within the time limit of a teacher's planning period, Teaching Excellence has created a flow for the debrief that takes 45 to 50 minutes.

A teacher should walk away from a debrief with:

- Clear knowledge of what they did well and should continue
- Clear knowledge of what needs to change
- Understanding of why it needs to change
- Practice in a replicable process for how it will change
- Motivation to implement the solution habitually

As a result, they will increase their skill level as teachers and the achievement of their students.

Structure

There are half a dozen important milestones to hit during a debrief. As the goal of a debrief is to further the skill of the teacher, the largest time slot is devoted to application and practice. The next most concentrated timeslot is allocated to glows and grows, each weighted evenly. The remaining elements include relationship building, logistics, and wrapping things up.

The Debrief

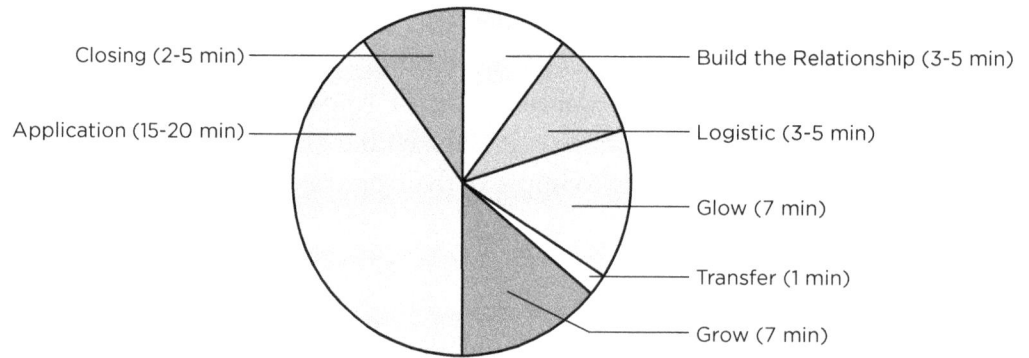

Closing (2-5 min) ——
Application (15-20 min) ——

—— Build the Relationship (3-5 min)
—— Logistic (3-5 min)
—— Glow (7 min)
—— Transfer (1 min)
—— Grow (7 min)

Build the Relationship

As mentioned in Chapter 2, "Building Teacher Relationships," growth thrives in a supportive, understanding environment. The connection between a teacher and their coach is vital to success. Establishing the relationship isn't a one-time event, but an ongoing process. It's imperative that you take time at the start of every conversation to check in on the well-being of the teacher. The debrief devotes the first three to five minutes to easing into the conversation and nurturing the relationship through asking questions and engaging in active listening. Cover their personal and professional life as appropriate, asking about highs and lows if they aren't forthcoming. You should gain more context with every interaction and use this context to tailor your feedback to their reality. If they have expressed in the past that a particular goal or practice is irrelevant to their situation, you're not going to win them over by suggesting it again without getting buy-in first. If, on the other hand, you're able to open with questions about life events, students, or situations a teacher has mentioned in the past, they see that you are building context for their classroom and are more likely to trust your feedback.

When you start the meeting by asking the teacher how things are going, you will get a wide variety of responses. There will be times you will need to empathize with their struggles. When appropriate, share anecdotes from your own personal experience so they know that difficult situations are a part of the first year of teaching, and that there are ways to grow from that struggle.

If a teacher becomes highly emotional or distracted by a situation, personal or professional, use your intuition to determine how long to discuss or attempt to resolve the issue. For example, if a teacher is stressed and hardly sleeping because they are trying to get everything done, they probably won't have energy to implement a teaching action step. You must address the issue before moving into coaching on a key lever. If the problem recurs over several debriefs, you'll need to have a conversation about their progress and potentially bring in other stakeholders to better support the teacher. If the teacher is going through an extremely difficult scenario, do what you can to get them the support they need.

If they are able to work through their situation, assure the teacher that while you care about them as a person, you also care about them as a professional and about their students. Therefore, you want to make sure you're reaching the intended outcome in each debrief.

Logistics

Once you have caught up with the teacher, direct the conversation to upcoming deadlines to verify that the teacher is aware of and prepared for any deliverables. Then ask about the outcomes of action steps from previous debriefs. This should take only a few minutes.

Sharing the Structure

Share the goal and structure of the meeting with the teacher at the outset of the meeting. For example, you can say, "We'll discuss strengths of the lesson, areas of growth for the lesson, and spend a significant portion of our time applying the new strategies. At the end of our time, I'd like to have a modified exit routine ready to roll out tomorrow."

The teacher may bring up something that is bothering them before you communicate the agenda. Make a judgment call about when to address the issue— immediately, at the end of the meeting, or at a future meeting—and settle it up front. For example, you can say:

- "Let's reserve ten minutes at the end of our time today to revisit that topic because I know it's important to you. "
- "This sounds like an issue that is weighing heavily on your mind. I actually came prepared to discuss some feedback directly related to that."
- "Thanks for bringing this issues to my attention. Let's address it right now since it's extremely sensitive/urgent."
- "That's a good question. Let me look into it and get back to you tomorrow."

Evidence Impact Statements

Evidence-impact statements are a type of cause-and-effect sentence which highlight the connection between a teacher's actions (the cause) and the effect on the classroom. Teachers are often focused mostly on themselves during a lesson. Evidence-impact statements help them shift their focus to students and understand how their instructional choices contribute to or detract from student learning. Your running notes record the evidence of what happened during the observation. The impact describes the effect on students. Using this formula for providing feedback helps teachers take ownership of their actions.

Sample evidence-impact statements:

- You asked three checks for understanding after you introduced new material. As a result, 70 percent of your students could answer the guided practice problems correctly.

- You stood next to table number two. As a result, the two off-task students stopped talking and began working on the assignment.
- You repeatedly posed questions to the class without stating expectations. As a result, five students consistently called out answers.
- You modeled the process for solving the problems by referencing student-friendly steps that were posted on an anchor chart. Students referenced this anchor chart to complete their work, and when asked, were able to pinpoint where in the process they were having difficulty.

An evidence-impact statement should draw a clear line from the evidence, to the impact on the students, to any corrective action. Here are some poorly formed evidence-impact statements:

Statement: "Four students were off task during guided practice. I wonder what we can do to differentiate instruction for the high flyers in your classroom."

Issue: There is no direct connection between "students off task" and "differentiating instruction for high flyers." You also know the solution for differentiating and will introduce it during the conversation.

Statement: "During group work, four out of five groups got stuck on problem number three and weren't sure how to proceed. Develop a system to notice these student misunderstandings and address them with the class."

Issue: Teachers need to see the link between their action, or lack of action, and its effect on students. The first sentence should address the teacher's action, for example, "You stayed at one table and didn't circulate during practice."

Glow

As that irrepressible sprite Mary Poppins observed, "A spoonful of sugar helps the medicine go down." Everyone is more receptive to a suggestion for improvement when it is preceded by a compliment.

A glow is a targeted piece of positive feedback regarding a teacher action that had a demonstrable or substantial impact on student learning. When possible, connect a glow to a grow from a previous debrief to demonstrate progress in the classroom.

A glow captures a behavior in the classroom that should be sustained and developed, that is making the biggest impact on the classroom, or that is just fun or exciting. Convey the glow in language that is familiar to the teacher, such as from professional development or from your campus or district's evaluative rubric.

State the glow using an evidence/impact format that combines a description of what the teacher did and the effect it had on student learning, supported by data. For example, you can say, "Because you stated expectations before starting the activity, the students were clear on what to do and 20 out of 22 successfully executed the gallery walk. Keep doing this each time you give directions!" Always make it clear that praise regarding a practice is not based on your preference, but on the impact to student outcomes. We want teachers to know that we are not looking for them to do teaching moves that we prefer, rather we promote actions that are impactful and increase student achievement.

Invite the teacher to give their own examples of what went well during the observation and ask follow-up questions, pushing them to explain how their actions led to the positive outcome. The teacher may notice something different from what you planned to use for a glow. If the teacher's example targets something that didn't go as well as they thought, first validate what went well and then highlight the aspect that could be improved.

Similarly, don't over-inflate how well the teacher is performing, mistaking an improvement for a strength. For instance, if a teacher communicated expectations but lacked clarity and specificity, it would be inappropriate to say, "Today you did a great job of stating expectations." You could instead point out that they have improved since the beginning of the year when they were not stating expectations at all using a specific data point.

Most teachers and professionals are highly motivated to improve, which means they often have the tendency to rush past what they're doing right and focus on what went wrong. Take the full time for glows. If the teacher seems uncomfortable with praise, resist the urge to move on to areas for growth. Spending time articulating what a teacher is doing well draws their attention to the parts of their practice they should keep doing. Teachers will alter many of the components of their pedagogical practice, particularly during their first year. It's important to highlight the elements that they should preserve. During a time in their career when they are learning so much, you want to make sure that teachers perform consistently the skills they already have. Effective teachers are constantly reflecting on their own practice. A novice teacher needs to cultivate the ability to recognize effective moves and replicating them.

Transfer

As you move from the glow to the grow, explicitly name the strengths that the teacher will need to rely on in order to improve in their growth area. In part, we bring up the teacher's strengths to tie in a sense of competence to take on the coming challenge to improve. For example, you might say, "Your key points have really improved and are now very clear to students. I want to leverage the planning skills you've developed with your key points. Let's explore how we can make practice just as clear and engaging."

If, during the build-the-relationship time, the teacher brought up struggles that relate to the grow you have selected, refer to it as evidence you are both aligned and in sync. For example, you could say, "I know you mentioned that students really struggled in the practice time today and that frustrated you because you thought the exercise would be easy for them. The main skill we need to work on today will impact students' practice directly."

At times there are quick fixes a teacher needs to make that are not connected to your key lever, but whenever possible, directly state the nature of connections that do occur. Connect the glow and grow by praising a specific teacher action, noting the impact on students, and then providing a quick tweak to increase the effectiveness of what the teacher did. For example, you could say, "Because you chunked the task and provided clear time limits, 100 percent of your class paced themselves well enough to complete the review. However, the students who finished quickly just sat there waiting while others labored over an answer. In the future, for this group you could have them collaborate with their neighbors and come to a consensus before writing the answer. This and the dual benefit of encouraging mentoring between peers, boosting student confidence and comprehension, while keeping the students occupied as a group until the practice is completed."

Grow

A grow is a targeted piece of feedback regarding an area for improvement; it is an explanation of the key lever you selected. Like strengths, areas for growth must be based on data and tied to teacher actions and their impact on student outcomes. As with the glow, the grow should reference a common rubric. For example, using the TE rubric, you would show how their actions match the "Ineffective" or "Somewhat Effective" levels, and then use the language of the "Effective" category to frame the goal for practice and application.

Pro-Tip: During the debrief, allow teachers who are self-reflective or possess sufficient experience the chance to suggest grows before you do. If necessary, ask follow-up questions to help the teacher explore how their actions led to the negative outcome in the classroom. Depending on whether the teacher notices the same issues that led you to the key lever for the debrief, there are three ways you can respond:

- Teacher self-identifies the key lever. "I also noticed that, and we will practice that skill today."
- Teacher self-identifies a legitimate grow related to the key lever. "I noticed that, and our practice today will help with that problem, although it may seem unrelated at first."
- Teacher self-identifies a legitimate grow that is not the key lever. "I noticed that too, but we're going to work on another issue today because [include explanation]. Perhaps we can address that [in some other appropriate way/time]."

After you have presented the grow, give the teacher time to respond. Sometimes this will happen automatically. Other times, you will need to ask a question to invite the feedback. For example, you could say, "How does this feedback land with you? How do you feel about this feedback?" Allow time for the teacher to process the evidence and help them understand the urgency and need to improve in the specified area. If the teacher has questions or reservations, continue to point to evidence from the lesson. Some teachers will immediately recognize the gap.

Pro-Tip: Know when to quit selling. You must continue to explain the gap and need for improvement until you get buy-in from the teacher and not a moment more. You may have more evidence, but there's no need to burden the teacher with more examples if they already agree with the key lever. Instead, use the gained time for practice.

Application and Practice

Application through practice lies at the heart of the debrief, and constitutes the bulk of the agenda. Because it's so important, we've devoted an entire chapter to practice alone. See Chapter 9, "Application and Practice," for more information.

Closing

In the final minutes of the debrief, recap the action steps you and the teacher have agreed upon and how they should demonstrate the skill moving forward, noting specifically what you will look for in the next observation session.

Then tell the teacher what you will do to follow up. For example, you can promise to return the following week to see the teacher executing the skill or request that the teacher email you to with a status update if you are unable to schedule an observation. Clarify what both you and the teacher need to do after the meeting is over. Let the teacher know if you are communicating with other stakeholders, like an evaluator or another campus administrator.

You can also use this time to address issues that came up at the beginning of the meeting, particularly if the teacher had a concern that was not resolved within the debrief.

The debrief is the heart of building excellence in a novice teacher, the crucible where they are confronted with the need for improvement and are given the opportunity to begin the process of skill building to better meet the needs of their students. It is a powerful tool that must be handled with deliberation and care on part of the teacher educator. As such, you must ensure that you set up teachers to be as successful as possible both during the debrief, and as they implement your feedback in following classes.

Appendix: Coaching Conversation Tools

Following are two resources you can use to plan your debrief meeting. Using these tools helps focus the conversation and ensure you reach the outcome you want within your time limit.

Teacher:	Date:
Goal:	Student Outcome:

Debrief Agenda

Time	Part of Debrief	Description
2 minutes	Opening	Small Talk/Greetings Sentence Stems/ Examples • How was your weekend? • How has your day been so far?
1 minute	Goal/Objective	What is the intended outcome of the meeting? For the next 45 minutes I would like to share with you some strengths and areas of growth that I observed that I believe will help to move you and your students forward...
3 minutes	Glow (with evidence)	What went well with evidence Sentence Stems/Examples • During the lesson, I saw... and the impact on your class was... • Keep doing this because...
1 minute	Connection to [evaluative rubric] (Specific Indicator)	Language from the [evaluative rubric] which supports your feedback
3 minutes	Glow (with evidence)	What went well with evidence Sentence Stems/Examples During the lesson, I saw... and the impact on your class was... Keep doing this because...
1 minute	Connection to [evaluative rubric] (Specific Indicator)	Language from the [evaluative rubric] which supports your feedback

Time	Part of Debrief	Description
1 minutes	Transfer	Connect the GLOW to the GROW (if possible) AND have the NT summarize their feedback Summarize: So, what are you doing well and why should you continue to do this? Move from the GLOW to the GROW: Your strength in lesson planning is an area I want to leverage as we talk about your area for growth.
4 minutes	Grow (with evidence)	What needs improvement with evidence Sentence Stems/Examples During the lesson, I saw... and the impact on your class was... This should be changed because...
1 minute	Connection [evaluative rubric]	Language from the [evaluative rubric] which supports your feedback
4 minutes	Grow (with evidence)	What needs improvement with evidence Sentence Stems/Examples During the lesson, I saw... and the impact on your class was... This should be changed because...
1 minute	Connection [evaluative rubric] (Specific Indicator)	Language from the [evaluative rubric] which supports your feedback
20 minutes	Practice/Application	Options for this time: Put this feedback into an upcoming lesson Have NT practice implementing the feedback (i.e. stating the expectation in a voice devoid of upspeak) Create resources to be used in next lesson or class

Time	Part of Debrief	Description
2 minutes	Questions, Thoughts, Pushback	Questions from the coach: Tell me your thoughts on this feedback Pre-planned anticipation of pushback Situational excuses ("it was an assembly schedule," "the kids were let out late from PE," etc) Pre-planned response to pushback Re-emphasis of why the feedback will help the students
1 minutes	Check for Understanding	Make sure that information has soaked in What were the two key things we talked about in the meeting? What will you use to plan out your lessons? What do you need to send me/your planning partner/ your dean?
2 minutes	Closing	Schedule next observation
47 minutes	Total	

Gut Instinct/ Big Ideas		
	Key Lever/ Catalyst →	* student achievement *observable student actions
Clarifying Questions (without laying blame, not assuming)	Connections (campus PD, TE workshops, previous meetings)	
Goal		
Topic for discussion	Specific objective for session	

Positive Feedback	
Evidence	[Rubric] Indicator(s)

Focus Areas for Growth		
Evidence	Key Lever/ Rubric Indicator	Criteria For Success / Questions
		1.
		2.
		3.

Transfer Strategies (using strengths to promote growth)	Wrap-up
	New teacher call to action:
	Follow-up:

1. During which portion of a debrief are you most susceptible to getting behind in your pacing? Personal exchanges at the beginning? Sharing rationale? Once you identify your own trouble-spots, what is an accountability system (e.g. time-stamps for each debrief segment) you could utilize to avoid tangents or prolonged coach-talk?

2. How much time is normally dedicated to application and practice during your debriefs with teachers? What needs to happen in the first part of a debrief in order to protect practice time?

3. Using precise language when coaching is critical. What are some of your positive catch-phrases – "You did an awesome job at…" or "_____ was really strong…"? Write a line or two of positive feedback to a teacher using evidence impact statements rather than your go-to phrase. How will this change your teacher's perception of the feedback you're sharing?

8

CHAPTER 8 **Criteria for Success**

"When it is obvious that the goals cannot be reached, don't adjust the goals, adjust the action steps" — Confucius

If the key lever is the "what" that comes out of a debrief with a teacher, criteria for success are the "how." Here, the phrase "Criteria for Success" refers to a formal record noting the necessary elements to successfully execute a strategy or teacher move. At YES Prep, we also encourage teachers to use criteria for success with students when describing an excellent output produced in class. In the same way, a coach's criteria for success should describe all the attributes of a teaching strategy done well so that the teacher has a clear picture of how their practice needs to change.

The criteria for success may, but do not necessarily have to, correspond to the steps in the process of executing the skill. Instead, they serve as a guide to highlight which foundational components must be present when the skill is executed. Many teacher moves can be performed in a variety of ways while adhering to the same criteria for success.

For example, suppose you're working with a seventh-grade math teacher toward the end of the first semester. This teacher has not yet mastered the skill of adjusting course after performing a check for understanding, but instead proceeds with the lesson even if students all answered the question wrong. You could define the following criteria for success:

An effective check-for-understanding process should:

- Stipulate that 100 percent of the students should answer the question
- Enable the teacher to quickly see all student responses to the question
- Determine thresholds for moving on, reviewing, or re-teaching the key point
- Have a pre-planned, specific move for reviewing or re-teaching

Using the criteria for success above, you then collaboratively formulate the check for understanding the teacher would implement. You would first decide with the teacher a method for getting all students to answer the questions visibly, like using whiteboards or asking multiple-choice questions using letter cards. You would then set thresholds with the teacher. For example, you could tell the teacher: "If more than half the class answers the question correctly, move on. If it's less than half, re-teach the key point." Last, you would introduce a strategy for re-teaching a key point, like introducing a different example.

Notice how the criteria for success are directly aligned to each specific action step while also leaving room for a variety of strategies to be used based on teacher preference. Letter cards are one way of ensuring 100 percent participation. Having students write their answers on a white board or even raising their hands for answer choice options are acceptable alternatives. Similarly, if the class size is small (fewer than 20 students), 75 percent of students may be too low of a threshold to move on. You and the teacher may decide to raise the threshold to 90 percent for small classes. Teachers with especially strong planning skills could chose to create separate practice sheets for different groups of students, depending on how successful they were with a series of checks for understanding.

Criteria for success can therefore be used to focus teachers' efforts while still giving them choice, and can be formatted in three ways:

3 types of criteria for success		
Format	**Description**	**Works well when the teacher**
Steps	Sequential list of moves a teacher should do	Needs to follow a process, and/or gets overwhelmed by choice
Checklist of attributes	Elements that should be present when executing the skill	Needs to embody certain characteristics such as authoritative presence, and/or prefers being involved in the decision making
Guiding questions	Prompts to guide the thought process behind executing the skill	Is planning a part of a lesson. Questions provide direction for the thinking process.

While there is no single way to write effective criteria for success, there are certain types of teaching skills and strategies that lend themselves more to one format than others. The examples provided in this chapter are not exhaustive, but should provide guidance and clarity regarding the most appropriate format.

Steps

Criteria for success written as steps are common for behavior management processes and teacher moves where there are clearly defined actions to take. Again, the criteria for success will provide guidance regarding the steps for successful execution, but do not prescribe exactly what the teacher must do.

In this first example, suppose you are supporting a teacher early in the school year who is having difficulty getting their students to quiet down and begin their work after the start of class.

Criteria for success example:

1. Use an attention-getting technique to pause the conversation.
2. Wait for 100-percent compliance, and redirect if necessary.
3. Re-state the expectations for work time, using a calm, authoritative voice.
4. Clearly release students to do their work.

The criteria for success used in this situation inform the teacher of the required steps, while also providing agency regarding which strategy to use to accomplish those steps. The teacher might have a preferred attention-getting technique, or you may suggest a new technique that is more appropriate than what they have been using. Starting with the attention-getter communicated as a required element, you and the teacher can collaborate on the nature of the remaining elements during the debrief.

Step-by-step criteria for success are also commonly used during academic planning processes that may be unfamiliar to a new teacher. In this example, suppose you are supporting a teacher who is preparing a reading passage, article or primary source that is above students' current reading levels.

Academic criteria for success example:

1. Read through the article two times.
   a. Read for yourself to understand the article
   b. Read while pretending to be a middle-of-the-road student.
2. Identify difficult vocabulary words that are necessary for understanding the text.
3. Make these vocabulary words accessible to your students: add footnotes with definitions, introduce the words at the beginning, or delete and paraphrase those words.
4. Identify big concepts that students must understand before they begin reading. Prepare to address those big ideas or concepts before they read the text, such as through a PowerPoint presentation or a discussion.
5. If possible, identify ways of re-leveling the text to be more reader-friendly.
   a. Delete or shorten overly-complex sentences/paragraphs.
   b. Use an online resource to level text.

The criteria for success in this example will serve this teacher in future planning because it is broadly applicable to any instance in which they might need to unpack an advanced text. Notice, too, that these criteria for success could be used for a teacher in any content, whether they teach science, history, or English Language Arts.

Sometimes there is no specific process a teacher must follow to implement a strategy, but rather a set of attributes that must be true. In this case, a checklist clearly communicates what you want to see in the classroom. A checklist is broadly applicable to certain behavior management or classroom culture-building strategies, as well as to academic or instructional skills.

Consider common criteria for success used to coach teachers struggling with classroom management due to a lack of authoritative presence and are exhibiting typical symptoms that you may see from a novice teacher. Students do not consistently listen when the teacher gives instructions. The teacher attempts to redirect misbehavior and issue consequences, but the students don't take them seriously.

Example: Authoritative presence

- Stand still and tall when speaking.
- Project your voice. Keep tone firm and emotionally neutral.
- Give directives. Do not phrase instructions as questions or requests.
- Use concise, behavior-focused language.

Consider another common instructional situation. A teacher has very little on their walls to support student learning, or the anchor charts they do have are ineffective (too small, too cluttered, too detailed, etc). The following criteria for success address the essential attributes of an effective instructional anchor chart.

Example: Creating an anchor chart

- Large enough to be seen from any seat in the class
- Referenced during delivery of key point or process explanation
- Employs visuals with minimal writing
- Symbols or color-coding so that individual components of the concept are recognizable at a glance

$$a^2 + b^2 = c^2$$

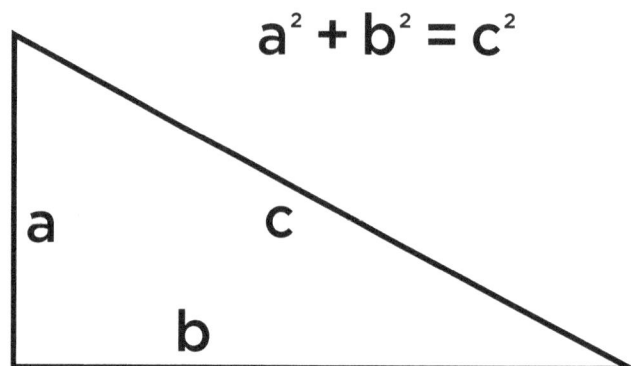

Guiding Questions

A series of guiding questions are commonly used to support the teacher's thought process while developing the implementation of a strategy to be applied in their classroom or incorporated into their lesson planning process. The goal is not to drive the teacher towards a specific right answer to the guiding questions, but rather to engage them with questions as they find a solution that will work best for their needs.

Suppose you are supporting a teacher who is ready to differentiate support for students in class. Notice how the following questions are structured such that, when a teacher answers one, it naturally flows into thinking about the next question.

Example: Differentiating student support

- Which of my students easily grasped the objective?
  - What is an extension I can give them?

- Which of my students are approaching mastery?
  - How can I provide them additional opportunities to solidify their understanding?

- Which of my students are struggling?
  - What is the barrier holding them back?
  - How can I explain the material in a new way?

Again, the purpose of asking and answering these questions is to give novice teachers an explicit structure for the types of planning and decision making that more experienced teachers do with greater ease. Now suppose you are supporting a teacher who plans to use a video to introduce new academic material. Notice how the questions are structured to help frame various considerations you want the teacher to account for in their planning process.

Example: Planning a video-driven lesson

- How is the video aligned to the objective and/or standard you are teaching?
- What are the gaps in the alignment and how can you fill those gaps succinctly?
- How will students process the video?
  - How will you frame the purpose for video to students prior to playing it?
  - When/how often will you pause for processing?
  - What questions will you ask students and how will they respond?
- What vocabulary do you need to unpack before students watch the video?

Coaching with Criteria for Success

The application domain of our coaching rubric (ICER) starts with language regarding the criteria for success.

95

	Application		
Not Meeting Expectations	**Approaching Proficiency**	**Proficient**	**Mastery**
Criteria for success are not stated.	Criteria for success are either not specific, not clear, or not directly aligned to the outcome.	Criteria for success are specific, clear, and directly aligned to the outcome.	In addition to the criteria listed in the proficiency column, • The process for implementing the action steps is made explicit such that the teacher will be able to replicate the underlying skill with fidelity.
During the meeting, the coach does not provide examples or model the criteria for success or does so unsuccessfully.	During the meeting, the coach attempts to provide examples of the criteria for success and/or models the criteria for success with mixed results.	During the meeting, the coach provides meaningful examples of the criteria for success and/or successfully models the criteria for success as appropriate.	
The novice teacher does not have the opportunity to apply the criteria for success.	The novice teacher has limited opportunities to apply the criteria for success and/or does not receive specific and strategic feedback.	The novice teacher has ample opportunities to apply the criteria for success and receives specific and strategic feedback.	
The coach and teacher do not discuss potential obstacles.	The coach and teacher discuss potential obstacles without reaching a resolution.	In order to ensure implementation, the coach and teacher discuss potential obstacles and problem solve in order to mitigate these obstacles.	
A specific timeline to implement the criteria for success is not suggested and the coach's follow-up is not articulated.	A specific timeline to implement the criteria for success is not suggested and/or the coach's follow-up is not articulated.	The coach and/or teacher suggests a timeline to implement the criteria for success. The coach's follow-up is articulated.	

The reason criteria-for-success are so pervasive in the application portion of the rubric is because having them as an anchor for each component of application increases the likelihood that the teacher will be able to successfully implement the key lever. And that's the whole point of the conversation.

Once the criteria for success are established, you must explicitly model it for the teacher demonstrating the skill while highlighting the criteria for success. You would stand and deliver a part of the lesson as if you are the teacher, or think aloud about what you're doing and why you're doing it as you plan a lesson. It is critical that the criteria for success drives the model. There are a variety of strategies you can use to ensure this happens.

One strategy is to explicitly name the criteria before you model, and then direct the teacher to identify where they saw each criterion after your model has concluded. This will enable you to check the teacher's understanding of the criteria for success, while also providing the teacher a processing opportunity before they practice themselves.

Similarly, and equally as important, the criteria for success should also drive the feedback that you provide to the teacher as they practice during the application portion of your debrief. As the teacher practices, point out the elements that are effective or aligned to the criteria for success and what they should change. This technique will hold you accountable for being concise with your feedback while also helping your teacher know exactly what elements of their practice they need to maintain and which they should focus in on for the next round.

For example, suppose you are having a teacher early in the year practice addressing the whole class with an authoritative presence using the criteria for success listed previously:

1. Use an attention-getting technique to pause the conversation.
2. Wait for 100-percent compliance, and redirect if necessary.
3. Re-state the expectations for work time, using a calm, authoritative voice.
4. Clearly release students to do their work.

Your feedback after the first round of practice may sounds like this:

"That time you used an effective attention getting technique, and you had a very clear release to let students know it was time to work. In this next round, make sure you project your voice and scan the room for 100-percent compliance. I purposefully looked at the seat next to me instead of you, and this went unaddressed. Taking three to five seconds to scan the room will let you address non-compliant behavior and communicate the message to your students that you will follow through on your expectations."

If the teacher's practice is ineffective, and the feedback they need is not aligned to the criteria for success, this could indicate that you need to add additional criteria. For example, if the teacher is planning a video-driven lesson (see above), it could be that the teacher chose a video that is not tightly related to the objective. In this case, you could add an initial question to serve as the first criterion: What key words or phrases in the objective should I use to search for a video?

It is also important to note that sometimes it is possible to use multiple sets of criteria within a single debrief. Using the above example, suppose the teacher executed all the criteria except speaking with an authoritative voice. You could introduce a second set of criteria for success around that specific speaking skill. In this way, an initial set of criteria may have nested within it disparate skills that have their own criteria for successful execution. This occurs most commonly when you are coaching on a holistic teaching skill or process–one that puts a series of skills to use in tandem.

For more information about running an effective application-based debrief, see Chapter 9, which discusses application.

"Criteria for Success" are the building blocks of an instructional practice that is sustainable and reproducible. The key lever acts as a gap that must be closed in a classroom and the criteria for success serve as the steps that a teacher must take to close that gap. Reflecting on the observation data, key lever, and criteria for success usually happens during a reflection period after the classroom observation. This work time may range from 20 to 45 minutes depending on your coaching experience. Once you have identified the data you will use, key lever you will coach on, the criteria for success required to implement the feedback, and the best way to structure your time with the teacher, you are now ready to execute your debrief conversation.

~ CHAPTER REFLECTION ~

1. What is the key lever for an upcoming debrief, or, for a teacher-move that you commonly coach on? Write out a criteria-for-success for this key lever. What format is most conducive? Where will you keep this information for future use?

2. Criteria for Success can also help more experienced teachers, especially when you collaboratively create the criteria. Who is an experienced or advanced teacher you support, and what is a teacher-move that you could discuss together in this fashion (e.g. what is the criteria for a successful Socratic circle)?

3. Are you and other instructional leaders on your campus/district normed on Criteria for Success for specific, common key levers? In other words, have you discussed with these colleagues what the elements of an effective check for understanding are, or the criteria for a successful teacher model? When is an opportunity to have this conversation?

$\bigcirc$
9

CHAPTER 9 **Application and Practice**

"Knowing is not enough, you must apply; willing is not enough, you must do." — Bruce Lee

At Teaching Excellence, we focus so intensely on practice because it increases the likelihood that novice teachers will implement a strategy and instinctively perform it well in their classroom. Practice encodes success. Consequently, application and practice constitute the bulk of the time in a debrief, taking 25 to 30 minutes for you to model the skill, observe the practice, provide feedback, and ideally have a second round of practice.

Elements of Application and Practice

Four elements make up the application and practice part of the debrief:

Criteria for success. Novice teachers have a much better chance of hitting the target if they know what they're aiming for. Develop criteria for success that describe the specific skill to practice and the metrics that reveal when the skill is done correctly. Present it at the beginning of the practice time. See Chapter 8: "Criteria for Success," for more information.

Model or exemplar. Model the skill or provide an example of the deliverable, linking each element to the criteria for success.

Practice. Have the teacher practice the skill in the low-stakes environment of a debrief to develop a feel for the rhythm of the skill before attempting it in the higher-stakes environment of the classroom. Repeat as many times as required.

Feedback. Provide feedback in the moment, based on the criteria for success, to refine their delivery.

The Criteria for Success

As discussed in Chapter 8, the criteria for success define the "how" of the skill—the steps or process that the novice teacher follows to master the skill that addresses the key lever for the debrief. There are three criteria-for-success formats:

99

Steps	Sequential list of moves a teacher should do
Checklist of attributes	Elements that should be present when executing the skill, such as posture, tone of voice, position in the room
Guiding questions	Prompts to guide the thought process behind executing the skill

The criteria for success anchors application. You will use the criteria for success to model the skill, whether in planning or in delivery. You will have the teacher look for those criteria for success. When the teacher stands up to practice, you'll use the criteria for success to give them feedback.

Pro-Tip: A best practice is to utilize resources from professional development sessions to create criteria for success. The key points of a session can often easily translate into steps, a checklist, or questions.

It is also important to note context for the specific teacher and classroom observation. Consider the observation data you collected and compare it to what would be ideal. Once you've identified the gap that exists, craft the criteria for success to address closing the gap.

In most cases, clearly defined criteria for success close a skill or knowledge gap for novice teachers. When you're working with an advanced teacher, you may be able to model reflective development by co-creating the criteria for success during the debrief using a model or example you have prepared. Discussing what makes for an effective classroom practice or element of curriculum can provide each of you an opportunity to share your experiences, beliefs, and values about specific educational practices.

Pro-Tip: You can save time by leveraging the criteria for success you develop for specific debriefs by collecting them in a document or folder. For example, if you create criteria for success to support a key lever regarding restorative conversation, there's a good chance you'll run across that issue in the future with another teacher. Hold onto it for future use.

The Model

Once you've identified the key lever for the debrief, selected an appropriate supporting strategy or skill, and created the criteria for success, your next step is to envision the execution of the skill in the novice teacher's context.

Execution-based lever

For an execution-based lever, such as behavior management or questioning strategies, plan the model with the teacher's classroom in mind. For example, if the observed issue is students talking back, then create a model for addressing that issue rather than some other less prominent behavior.

Consider how these two contexts would influence your choice of model when the key lever focuses on turn-and-talk.

Context	Model
Students are eager to talk and readily engage in academic conversations	Set clear expectations for starting and stopping the conversation
Students are not eager to talk, perhaps there is a high percentage of students who are developing their English language skills	Provide sentence stems and allow more time for conversation

During your model, the coach would stand and deliver the lesson as if they were the teacher in that classroom (even though the room is empty), incorporating the skill and explicitly highlighting the criteria for success. Model the skill with all the energy and focus you would use in a classroom full of students. If you have specific context for individual students or class periods, feel free to incorporate those into the model. Some people can perform when they have an audience, such as a room full of students, but become self-conscious when pretending to do the same thing on demand for an audience of one. If you are among this group, you will have to embrace your inner thespian and dance like nobody's watching when it's time to model a move. In fact, it can be helpful to admit the awkwardness up front, because then the novice teacher sees that you are modeling not only the skill but also the authenticity of the practice you're looking for. Seeing you do this will increase the authenticity that they bring when it's their turn.

Planning-based lever

For a planning-based lever, you can model by thinking aloud as you work through the process, posing the questions you ask yourself when working on the skill and connecting it to the criteria for success. You can also work through an existing lesson, correlating elements to the criteria for success.

Assemble your planning resources in advance. If the novice teacher's content area differs from your own, don't shy from using familiar content in the interest of efficiency, as long as the process is transferable. In other words, if you're supporting a physics teacher, but your teaching background is in geography, use your content expertise to model and show your teacher the clear transfer to their own subject. Talk about how your exemplar meets the criteria for success and actually walk through the planning process while thinking aloud for the teacher.

Pro-Tip: Use the teacher's lesson from that day for the model, and then have them practice with the lesson for tomorrow or future days.

Practice and Feedback

After modeling the skill, have the teacher apply it in a similar scenario: re-doing a portion of a lesson from the observation, another problem from the lesson you modeled, or a portion of an upcoming lesson. To increase authenticity, consider having the teacher use specific class periods, specific student names, or specific instances from the observation to recreate the classroom environment as closely as possible. Because we want this practice to translate as easily as possible into a teacher's classroom, we also encourage our teachers to adopt their in-class body language, which often includes standing and slowly moving around the room while they practice a skill.

Provide immediate feedback after the first practice run, prioritizing elements related to the criteria for success, followed by other issues you might have noticed during practice. If a bad habit crops up that you want to mitigate, amend the criteria for success in the moment to address this. For example, for a behavior management lever focused on setting expectations, if you notice the novice teacher being timid, you could embed a second set of criteria for addressing students with an authoritative voice.

If practice is way off, intervene, reiterate the criteria for success or model a specific portion a second time, and have them restart.

After providing feedback, have the teacher practice again incorporating the change. You are pushing the teacher to proficiency, so work through additional iterations until you are confident that the teacher can replicate the skill with fidelity, meaning that they hit each element of the criteria for success.

If time and progress permits, you can gradually escalate the context. For example, for a behavior modification lever, the first practice could reflect a compliant class, the second a class with a couple of misbehaving students, and the third a more significant management scenario.

At the end of the practice session, wrap up by asking the teacher to reflect on take-aways from the debrief.

You should always consider potential obstacles to implementation. The teacher may bring them up on their own, with a question that begins, "What if this happens?" If not, have them consider potential obstacles using questions such as:

- How do you need to modify this to work for third period?
- What about this is going to be most difficult to do when you plan on your own?

Pro-Tip: Complete all the work necessary to make the new skill happen during the debrief. For example, if it's a planning skill, during practice have the teacher adapt a lesson plan for the next day instead of saying, "Make sure you plan that in for tomorrow." Teachers should not feel that a meeting with you will always result in adding a to-do item in their schedule.

Occasionally you will need to substitute the skill to practice with another at the last minute. For example, suppose you notice during the observation that students are not getting to work right away during practice. You plan to coach on creating a sense of urgency—setting timers and transitioning quickly. Then during the debrief, the teacher explains that the actual problem is that the students aren't grasping the material, and she has to take time for remediation. In that case, you might choose to adjust practice on the fly to address the root cause (clarity of presentation) rather than the symptom (a sense of urgency). Even if you have to change your practice in the midst of a debrief, always recreate the core elements: criteria for success, model, and multiple opportunities for the teacher to apply the new skill.

Follow-up

Be very clear regarding follow up, i.e. explain what will happen next and when it will happen. For example, share when you will:

- Observe the implementation
- Provide additional resources
- Connect to another person, i.e. district content specialist, veteran teacher
- Provide answers to questions you couldn't address in the debrief
- Give feedback on the lesson plan, for a planning lever

Because application and practice allow a novice teacher to fail and improve in a safe place, they are essential components of growth and mastery. While it may feel awkward at first, both the novice teacher and the teacher educator must push through this insecurity to ease the implementation of a new skill in the classroom. The alternative is for the novice teacher to experience this trial and error process of experimentation in the classroom, which seldom results in the change hoped for by the teacher educator — or the students!

~ CHAPTER REFLECTION ~

1. Think of an upcoming debrief. How will you model the target skill or provide an exemple of what you want the teacher to produce? What is your criteria for success on this skill or process?

2. In this same debrief, once the teacher practices successfully, what is an appropriate barrier to implementation that you can introduce for another round of practice? A difficult class or student? A perplexing content concept? Or is it best to ask the teacher themselves what obstacles they anticipate might come up?

3. To ensure you have sufficient practice time, use the elements of a debrief information from this chapter to help create an agenda with timestamps for your coaching conversation. This can help you stay on track, especially if you or the teacher are prone to tangents.

10

CHAPTER 10   Additional Considerations During a Debrief

"Teaching players during practices was what coaching was all about to me." – John Wooden

Following the structure laid out up to this point, a teacher educator has put a tremendous amount of time and energy into safeguarding the effectiveness of the time spent with the teacher in a debrief. Time has been spent diagnosing a classroom, determining a key lever, breaking that key lever down into criteria for success, and then determining what a suitable practice would be to get the teacher appropriate practice with aligned skills. One would be wise, then, to do everything they can to make sure that the debrief itself results in the desired change; that teachers are invested in learning strategies that address the key lever, and that they are clear on how to apply those strategies in their classroom. This chapter provides some additional best practices that our coaches regularly use in order to increase the success rate of their debriefs and ensure that they get the best return on the investment of time that both they and their teachers make.

This chapter is organized into two domains of consideration: general coaching considerations that are widely applicable across coaching interactions, and considerations which are more specific to a teacher's individual context.

Coaching Considerations

Logistics

The Right Place

A debrief is a time of vulnerability for both the teacher and you. Privacy is essential.

In most cases, debrief meetings will take place on the teacher's campus rather than in your private office, assuming you're blessed with a private office. The best option is to meet in the teacher's classroom during a free period. This arrangement provides complete privacy and increases the authenticity of application and practice.

Either way, to cover your bases, it's a good idea to identify and vet possible meeting places at the beginning of the year. If the campus has a reservation system, use it. There's no guarantee that you won't be preempted by a last-minute priority, such as a parent-teacher conference, but it increases the odds of privacy.

In a pinch, a common area such as the library or cafeteria can serve as long as you can find a secluded corner.

The Right Time

The debrief should occur while the observation is fresh in everyone's memory. Within 48 hours of the observation is optimum. Sometimes an obligation or an emergency will conflict with the scheduled time. If possible, reschedule the meeting within 48 hours of the observation. If that's not possible, it's best to reboot and schedule a new observation and debrief.

A debrief should last 45 to 50 minutes. When a teacher is short on time, such as when they need to make copies for an upcoming lesson, you might be tempted to rush through the debrief in the time left. But there is a reason the debrief structure has a minimum of 45 minutes. Any less and you'll compromise the effectiveness of the touchpoint, usually because of insufficient practice time. Always confirm that the teacher can meet for the full session. If something comes up in the middle of a debrief, find a time you can finish to ensure that adequate time was spent discussing and practicing the key lever.

Direct Tone & Language

Effective coaches balance the "what you say" with the "how you say it" to get right at the heart of the classroom and accelerate teacher effectiveness. At Teaching Excellence, we account for these elements of a strong coaching conversation through an ICER rubric strand called Direct Tone and Language.

	Direct Tone and Language		
Not Meeting Expectations	**Approaching Proficiency**	**Proficient**	**Mastery**
The coach does not use direct language, compelling rationale, or relevant data.	The coach uses indirect language or data that is at times unclear or misaligned.	The coach uses precise and direct language, compelling rationale, and/ or relevant data in order to instill urgency in the teacher.	**In addition to the criteria listed in the proficiency column,** • The coach uses precise and direct language, compelling rationale, and relevant data in order to instill urgency in the teacher. • The coach's consistent use of direct language leads to an observably efficient use of time whereby additional time is created for application and reflection.
Tone used in conversation is combative, disrespectful, and/or not the appropriate level of urgency for the conversation.	At times, the coach uses a tone that is not confident or assertive (fillers, uptalk).	The coach uses a confident and assertive tone.	
If the teacher offers pushback, the coach does not address it or does so inappropriately.	If the teacher offers pushback, the coach attempts to address it with mixed results.	If the teacher offers pushback, the coach addresses it.	
The coach does not use wait time to allow for teacher processing (consistently interrupts teachers, answers own questions)	The coach attempts to use wait time in order to allow for teacher processing, with mixed results.	The coach uses wait time in order to allow for teacher processing.	

Effective teacher educators need to be direct with the teachers they support—sharing exact observations about strengths and growth areas in the classroom and providing evidence for how these actions are currently impacting student achievement. A masterful coach will use a variety of strategies to ensure that the conversation moves forward productively and that the coach and teacher don't end up talking circles around a particular issue.

Because of social norms, we are often unaccustomed to being as direct with people in our everyday interactions as teachers need a coach to be when providing feedback on their performance. Suppose, for example, a science teacher is long-winded and their explanations in class contain too many tangents such that students get confused. Well-intentioned teacher educators might say something like, "your explanation of the cell division process was thorough, but I think students still had a lot of questions when they had to start their work," hoping to soften the blow and spare the teacher's feelings. The problem with ambiguous phrasing like this is that it invites doubt about the actual need to change. Conversations that start like this can often result in the teacher and coach only talking about the issue, or the observed lesson, instead of focusing on how to fix the problem and avoid the issue in future lessons.

Precise, direct language enables the coach to get right to the point, perhaps saying instead: "Your explanation of cell division was confusing because you shared so many anecdotes, and as a result, only seven of the 23 students in your class were able to start on their independent assignment." This gets to the heart of the issue and states on no uncertain terms what the coach is attempting to address going forward. Time otherwise spent discussing the situation, can now be spent practicing a new skill to prevent the situation from occurring again. Being direct isn't about being hyper-assertive or critical—these actions will damage your relationship with your teacher. Using direct language to share feedback is about simply stating what specifically needs to change. Be mindful of your tone of voice. Having a problem in the classroom doesn't make your teacher a bad person, and they shouldn't feel this way either! State your feedback matter-of-factly, and with an attitude of support. After all, while you're providing feedback on their teacher moves, you're also helping them train to make those teacher moves stronger.

Notice that the last bullet point in the proficiency column of direct tone and language has to do with wait time. In other words, a good coach needs to know when to stop talking as well, and let the teacher think. As you read more about questioning strategies later in this chapter, remember this point about processing time, as silence from you, the coach, is a great follow up when you ask a good question.

Anticipate Pushback

The best way to resolve objections to a course of action is to anticipate them and address them before they are raised. Based on what you know about the teacher, can you foresee likely roadblocks to buy-in? If so, how can you plan your presentation to pre-emptively remove them? Making suggestions that the teacher cannot envision without discussing the possible issues can prompt the teacher to dis-invest in the key lever.

One way to preempt objections is to create a set of questions related to overall classroom context that drill down to the specific key lever targeted for the debrief that lead the teacher to the gap and the need to bridge it.

Using Rationale to Ensure Buy-In

Teachers want their students to succeed. It is no surprise then, that the strongest link to establishing teacher buy-in is often a clear and compelling rationale tied to student achievement. In addition, you should review your key lever in the light of all you know about a teacher, their strengths, weaknesses, and personal teaching style, to frame it in a manner that is compatible with their personality and values.

Questioning

There is an art to questioning, as anyone who has asked, "Are you going out wearing that?" can attest to.

Trial lawyers are advised to never ask a question if they don't already know the answer. For the coach, the situation is reversed. You should never ask a question if you already know the answer. For example, "What should you have done instead of repeatedly redirecting the same student?" If you know the answer, then drop the question and just state the fact. "Instead of repeatedly redirecting the same student, you should have imposed a consequence." In general, avoid asking a teacher, especially a novice, "What do you think you can do to improve in this area?" If they knew how to improve, they wouldn't need a coach.

Properly framed questions honor the teacher as a person, unlock the information within the teacher, increase buy-in and establish authenticity.

Ask questions to discover information:

- When this situation occurs, what do you typically do?
- Is your response to this situation normal for your classroom?
- What about that particular practice resonates with you?

As the teacher develops during the academic year and gains proficiency, the debrief will take on a more conversational tone. You can use questioning to increase the effectiveness of your debrief, particularly in situations where you notice that feedback is implemented sporadically or incorrectly. This gap may stem from a lack of input from the teacher. Conversely, you may see feedback implemented, but aren't sure that the teacher understands the rationale for the skill. They shouldn't be using a skill just because you said so.

The TE Instructional Coaching Excellence Rubric (ICER) looks for four elements of proficiency in questioning:

Questioning			
Not Meeting Expectations	**Approaching Proficiency**	**Proficient**	**Mastery**
Few or no questions are asked which affects the investment of the novice teacher in the conversation.	The coach attempts to use questioning to invest the novice teacher in the conversation, though does not employ a variety of strategies.	The coach uses a variety of questioning strategies to invest the novice teacher in the conversation.	**In addition to the criteria listed in the proficiency column,** • The coach uses a variety of questioning strategies to *get at the core driver of teacher and/or student behavior* (why the behavior is happening). • The coach moves away from scripted questions because the level of engagement and genuine curiosity lead to customized reflection on the part of the teacher.
Open-ended questions are not used.	Open-ended questions are present but at times are not strategic (overly scripted).	Open-ended questions are strategic (to involve data, to allow reflection, to uncover mindsets, to encourage participation of novice teacher in the development of action steps)	
The coach asks several leading questions which affects the teacher's participation in the debrief.	The coach asks some leading questions rather than questioning for the sake of seeking understanding.	The coach strategically uses questions to seek to understand.	
Most of the conversation is dominated by the coach which leads to a lack of teacher processing and engagement.	Parts of the conversation are dominated by the coach which leads to limited teacher processing and engagement.	The conversation is balanced and leans more towards focused teacher processing and engagement.	

A strategic question allows teachers to think about how they would apply the strategies and feedback in their current context and reflect on their current practice in the classroom. Coaches can also ask questions to gain clarity about necessary information that was not witnessed during the observation. This is the ARC method of questioning: apply, reflect, clarify.

For a question to be strategic you must ask at the right time. ARC questions are not necessarily asked in that (acronym) order. For example, include clarifying questions at the beginning of the debrief to avoid assumptions. Include a reflection question after you deliver the grows. Apply questions belong in the practice section of the debrief. You can start by scripting questions into your debrief. As you practice, you internalize good questioning strategies and begin to spontaneously form curious, authentic questions.

Application

Ask questions to help the teacher visualize what an application of the strategies looks like and how it affects their classroom, to uncover potential obstacles or concerns, and to motivate the teacher to follow through with application.

- What tweaks do we need to make to ensure this strategy runs smoothly in _____ period?
- When you do this process tomorrow, walk me through what you will do.
- What gets you most excited about implementing _____?
- If you were to implement this tomorrow, which class would struggle the most with the directions?
- Considering where your class is now, what would prevent you from beginning _____ next period/tomorrow?
- What do you anticipate the impact of this strategy will be on your low-performing students when you implement it?
- Which specific student(s) will benefit most as a result of this new strategy?
- Walk me through how this would look with your content.
- What else will you need to do to complete this action step?
- What support do you need to accomplish this?
- How can you put this all together?

Reflection

Ask questions to help the teacher reflect on their current or past practices and decisions in the classroom, the effects of those actions, and how they can replicate or change their current practices. The goal is to build a reflective practitioner who can continue to improve their teaching independently.

- What resonates with you about this feedback?
- What led up to you being able to successfully execute ____ today?
- How does this fit in with the vision for your class/your school/your grade level?
- What have you done in the past in similar situations?

- Think of a lesson where 3rd period was at its best. What did you do differently in that lesson? Why do you think they behaved well during that lesson?
- What part do you think you played in that situation?
- What is the opportunity/what is the challenge here?
- What is your desired outcome?
- What is holding you back?
- How is this different/similar than what you have done in the past?
- Knowing your strengths and weakness what will be the most difficult for you? What will come the most naturally?
- What was the tipping point for this change to happen?
- What changed?

Clarification

Ask questions to avoid making assumptions and to gain context.

- What factors did you consider when you decided to _____?
- What are the expectations for your teams?
- Tell me more about _____ student.
- Is _____ typical in all of your classes?
- Background: what led up to _____?
- What do you mean when you said _____?
- Walk me through the thought process that led to pulling that small group.
- What was going through you head during _____ part of class?
- What have you tried so far?
- Have you tried this strategy before? How did it go?
- How did you modify this lesson as you were internalizing to ensure it met the needs of your students?

Teacher considerations

Teacher Preferences

Key Question: What do I know about this teacher as a person?

Based on the personality of the teacher and your experience with previous debriefs, you should tailor your feedback to minimize negative reactions and maximize buy-in. Some teachers may do better when you soften the blow of critical classroom feedback, while others may need a stiff reality check to make them aware of their need for growth. Different teachers may prefer data points, stories from your own career, or a connection to individual students.

Capacity for Change

Key Question: Do I need to broaden or narrow the scope of my feedback?

One teacher may become overwhelmed by the same level of feedback that might invigorate another teacher. A teacher's capacity for implementing feedback should affect the balance between directness and questioning during the debrief. An overwhelmed teacher likely needs narrow, specific changes, whereas a teacher who is motivated by feedback might prefer broader change with more opportunity to offer input.

Emotional Responses

Occasionally when you present an area for growth, you will get a strong emotional response from a teacher. This often happens at the beginning of the year as a teacher is adjusting to the high volume of work expected of teachers and can be a result of the discomfort of receiving regular feedback about their work. If you think this is possible for a specific debrief, plan time in the agenda to address it.

First you should acknowledge the emotion with understanding and empathy. Dr. Ralph Nichols, pioneer in the field of listening, noted that the most basic of all human needs is the need to understand and be understood. Giving the teacher space to express their feelings and be heard is the first step toward addressing their concerns.

If there's a serious need in play, such as the teacher is staying up late planning or grading and isn't sleeping, you may need to address time management or planning skills leading to that problem. Use your best judgment regarding whether to proceed with the debrief, change your key lever, or reschedule the meeting altogether. If they can gain their composure, move forward with care.

Long-Term Development

Key Question: How does the key lever based on the current observation relate to their long-term development?

Once a teacher has demonstrated growth in an area, consult the rubric to investigate skills in the next band of their developmental trajectory. While telling teachers how they have grown over the year (formally in an evaluative sense) is always compelling rationale, it is also critical to know what their personal goals are as an educator. What kind of teacher do they want to be? Is there someone from their own experience that they aspire to emulate in the classroom? What does this teacher want to achieve in their second (or subsequent) school year? As a teacher educator, you have the knowledge to help teachers set these types of goals and plan out a sequence for their development in order to achieve them.

Instructional Goals

Key Question: Does this teacher have personal instructional goals?

A struggling novice teacher may not be ready to establish a goal beyond surviving the first year, but second and third year teachers should have vision for their career.

Look for a way to choose a key lever that will enhance efforts toward building their future as an educator.

Recent Evaluations

Key Question: Can you connect the details of your observation to a recent or upcoming evaluation from you or a campus evaluator?

If you are the evaluator, then you will already be comparing the details of the observation to previous scores. If you are not the evaluator, you should align your goals to the evaluator's trajectory. For example, the campus evaluator may expect all English teachers to execute strong modeling practices on book annotations during the fall semester and may establish this practice as a system-wide goal for novice teacher development.

Growth Plan

Key Question: Does this teacher have an improvement plan?

You or the campus administrator may have established a growth plan for the teacher that mandates improvement in specific, demonstrable ways that is tied to specific consequences. If this is the case, then for the sake of the teacher's career you need to map your developmental goal for the debrief to the expectations of the growth plan. They need not be mutually exclusive. The improvement plan should be prioritized, but it should also contain specific, desired teacher-actions. If the document does not specific concrete actions for the teacher to implement, then as the coach you should seek clarity from whoever drafted the document. While teachers never feel excited about being on such plans, coaching them on items listed in a growth plan can make them feel reassured and supported.

Going Forward

As you may have noticed, the purpose of these strategies and considerations is to remove barriers to implementation – whether they be real or imagined – so that changes in teacher actions can result in positive changes in student outcomes. The lion's share of the time, the best way to accomplish this change is through the traditional observation-debrief structure that we have focused on up to this point. However, sometimes, in order to effect the most change in the least amount of time, a different structure is called for. The next three chapters will introduce you to other techniques our teacher educators employ when they deem it appropriate.

1. What type of rationale do you rely on most frequently? How can you differentiate the rationale you provide based on your perceived teacher-needs?

2. Look at the list of suggested application and reflection questions. Which of these questions could you use in an upcoming debrief to shift more of the coaching conversation towards teacher processing and engagement rather than coach-talk?

3. Which of the teacher context considerations would make the greatest impact on your cohort if you were to adopt it into your practice?

11

Alternate Touchpoints

....

"Over every mountain there is a path, although it may not be seen from the valley."

— Theodore Roethke

It is no accident that the classic touchpoint in coaching novice teachers is a classroom observation followed by a debrief. This formula works for the majority of teacher education issues the majority of the time. However, when it comes to dealing with the human condition, one size certainly does not fit all. As a teacher educator, you must be sensitive to situations that require differentiated support. Your intuition may be based on student needs, specific classroom context, a teacher's personality, or their learning style. Often, an alternate touchpoint can tip the scales for teacher buy-in on an issue you've been addressing for some time without the results that you or your teacher would expect to see. These touchpoints can also be a tool for customizing individual support for teachers who are performing well. Rather than always responding to an observation, you can use alternate touchpoints to proactively further a teacher's development.

Video Observation
....

The video observation takes advantage of technology to allow the teacher to observe their lesson delivery in the classroom and its effect on the students. The video can include not only the teacher's presentation of one or more elements of a lesson plan, but also interviews with students about their experiences.

This touchpoint is especially helpful in cases where a teacher's self-perception and the reality of their effectiveness in the classroom are at odds, such as when a teacher:

- Is reluctant to implement feedback from previous meetings
- Believes things are going better than they really are
- Believes things are much worse than they really are
- Perceives that they are implementing a strategy effectively but is still missing the mark

A video observation can also help teachers who lack that crucial level of "with-it-ness" and simply don't notice the effect their action, or inaction, is having on students. The reality conveyed by an impartial third eye can spur the impetus the teacher needs to acknowledge that something isn't working (or that their perception of the classroom is inaccurate) and that change is imperative to their success in the classroom and in their career.

Because of the use of video, you will need to address logistics that don't come up in a traditional touchpoint. You must verify that you have permission to film, even if no one sees the result except you and the teacher. A small web-cam that can clip onto a laptop is less intrusive than a camcorder or a phone that you must carry and aim. The presence of a camera often causes students to act differently than they normally would, for better or worse. In that case, you may ask the teacher to announce to the class why they are being filmed. A simple explanation about how the teacher themselves has a person who helps them improve should suffice.

Pro tip: If your presence filming might cause a significant enough disruption to the classroom such that the video will not be useful, try the following strategy: Be ready in a student-free part of class (often the teacher's desk) before the students enter, and have your web-cam set up on your laptop. When class begins, act as you normally would in an observation for a few minutes. Then, leaving your cam appropriately aimed, step out of the classroom. Even if they are aware of the camera, students will often return to business as usual because you've removed yourself from the situation. After 10 to 15 minutes, return to retrieve your equipment.

Once you have your footage, watch the video before the debrief to take notes that will enable you to maximize the impact of the touchpoint. You will likely not watch the entire video with the teacher, but only certain snippets that highlight the key lever. Mark timestamps that you think are most critical, and/or identify a three- to five-minute portion of the video that best illustrates the need for the key lever you have selected. The rest of the debrief can be used for practice and application.

You will need to decide if you want the teacher to review the video on their own before you meet or if you want to review it with them during the debrief. If you want the teacher to watch it independently, identify elements to watch for in the video and when they occur. For example, if with-it-ness is a key lever for the teacher, you may instruct them to watch a five-minute section (timestamp 09:30 – 14:30, for example) and identify how many off-task student behaviors they see and whether or not they addressed the behaviors. Compare your notes with theirs in the debrief, and then discuss strategies for improvement. Allowing the teacher to see the video before the debrief can be helpful for teachers who may feel overwhelmed or anxious about seeing their own classroom. If you decide to review the video with the teacher, have a clear plan of what you are watching, what the key lever is, and what you want the teacher to take away from the experience. Because you have already screened the video, be prepared to draw their attention to specific students, specific teacher actions (or lack of action), and any other pertinent observable data to support your key lever.

In the beginning of the school year, it can be helpful for new teachers to see video of their students during some type of routine or transition. Elementary teachers may film students lining up to leave the classroom, science teachers may film their first lab day, or a P.E. teacher might film a class's warm-up routine. However, video observations are not just a tool for improving classroom management, they can also assist in improving clarity of academic instruction. For example, if a math teacher is unaware that they are struggling with their introduction to new material, you could review video of this portion of their lesson together with both of you adopting the perspective of students in the class trying to follow along. It is often helpful to film a teacher's modeling of a skill in class to identify strengths and weaknesses in clarity of explanations and how students respond to that in the moment. Videos are excellent tools for reflection when a teacher is implementing an academic routine (such as Socratic seminars) for the first time as well. Reviewing the lesson together will help you identify positive trends and elements as well as items to improve upon in future lessons.

Focus Lesson

In a focus lesson, you teach a lesson, or part of a lesson, while the novice teacher observes and takes notes. It is often helpful to have a short pre-conference to norm on the skill you will model, what the teacher should do during this time, and what they should look for. None of the elements of the focus lesson should come as a surprise to anyone.

This touchpoint is useful when you think a teacher will benefit from seeing a specific skill executed in real-time in their own classroom with their own students. It is especially helpful when you've been working on a skill for some time but haven't seen traction with the teacher. For example, a history teacher may be struggling to present a clear think-aloud for their students about how to analyze a historic political cartoon. Coming in as a guest-teacher and modeling an effective think-aloud with their students will provide a clear example of how to execute the skill and a salient connection on how this positively impacts student understanding of the content—perhaps reducing the amount of time the teacher spends clarifying concepts during student practice.

In the first meeting, establish the day, the period, and the skill you want to model while viewing the lesson plan for the day of the observation. You should also discuss how the teacher will explain your guest teaching to the students (who probably recognize you from previous observations and interactions). As the teacher educator, you may write the lesson plan yourself if planning is an issue. You can also ask the teacher to plan the bulk of the lesson, with some edits by you. When you are editing, record your thoughts so that they can be informative to your teacher. For example, you can highlight where in the lesson you will model the skill and (thinking out loud as you revise that element of the lesson plan) write notes communicating exactly what you want the teacher to focus on during the respective lesson. You can maximize the effectiveness of the following debrief if you outline the criteria for success you want the teacher to look for.

Pro-tip: Think carefully before doing a focus lesson in a classroom with behavior management concerns. Student-teacher relationships are core to teaching. If you take over a classroom for a focus lesson, make sure you have a solid relationship with the students to assure that you can demonstrate the skill in that environment. A focus lesson that fails can potentially shake the foundations of trust between you and that teacher. Your lesson delivery does not need to be perfect, but it does need to be proficient no matter what skill you're trying to impart.

Co-observation

In a co-observation, you and the teacher observe a more skillful teacher either at their school or at a different campus. In a situation where a teacher has developed a negative view of the students in a class and another teacher can achieve different results, this exercise can model execution and serve to change their mindset when they see the students respond to the instruction of a more experienced and perceptive teacher.

This touchpoint is especially applicable for teachers who learn best by observing and in situations where a teacher is struggling to visualize how to execute a strategy you've been advocating and modeling with traditional debriefs. It can also be helpful when you have a teacher who needs to see their grade-level and content being taught well (with a specific strategy in mind), but you don't have expertise in the content area.

Selecting the right teacher to observe is dependent on the specific skill you are trying to develop in the novice teacher. Leverage your knowledge of teachers' strengths. If you cannot identify someone on your own, reach out to others on your campus or in your district to find a good fit for the skill you have in mind. Be careful of the tendency to want to observe the best of the best. A novice teacher might see some amazing and inspiring instruction happening, but could simultaneously feel overwhelmed at the prospect of having to perform at that same level. A best practice is to observe a teacher with an attainable level of proficiency with that skill; often teachers in their second to fourth year of experience are a good fit. Take care to select a teacher with a temperament compatible with the novice teacher. For example, a calm and soft-spoken novice teacher who needs to learn how to manage students will have difficulty visualizing how to implement a skill that is modeled by a more animated, dynamic teacher.

A co-observation requires considerable planning and coordination, especially if you and the novice teacher must travel to a different campus. If travel is required, check with your teacher's admin to verify that they can take the time away from campus. If possible, schedule the observation during the novice teacher's planning period. If that isn't possible, arrange time off for professional development for the novice teacher and a substitute to cover any classes they will miss because of the observation.

Send out a calendar invite to everyone involved in the observation to assure that they block out the time. Ask the experienced teacher to attend the debrief, if possible, to answer questions and explain how they developed the skill you observed. After the touchpoint, co-write a thank-you note with the novice teacher to the experienced teacher, listing one or more positive take-aways the novice teacher gleaned from the experience. In the debrief or in a future session, collaborate with your novice teacher to map out action steps to implement the modeled skills.

Mindset Conversation

A mindset is a person's established set of attitudes and beliefs. While it is not our goal for teachers to have the same attitudes and beliefs of their coach, we know that there are some attitudes, beliefs, and behaviors that can be damaging for students. Because it can cross over into the teacher's sense of self, the mindset conversation is arguably the most powerful touchpoint you can employ. For that reason, it can also become the most volatile touchpoint if not handled carefully.

Indicators

During the normal course of coaching, you will often address a mindset issue on the fly as you respond to statements from the teacher, such as when a teacher says that they don't have time to provide a deliverable or that it doesn't apply to them or is outside their responsibilities. For example, a teacher may say that they don't feel they need to plan lessons fully in advance because they're able to execute well on the fly. The teacher may make a comment that contradicts best practices, such as that teaching by instinct provides better results than following best practices based on data.

Most crucial is when teachers push responsibility for performance issues onto others with statements such as

- "These kids…"
- "These parents…"
- "This community…"
- "The rest of my grade level…"
- "My co-planner wrote this lesson plan," etc.

These comments may reveal a teacher's bias regarding their students, colleagues, or the community they serve. Effective teaching begins with the mindset that teachers are responsible for everything that happens in their classroom, and their students are capable of anything they put their mind to.

Pay attention to these indicators that a formal mindset conversation touchpoint should be scheduled.

- Defensiveness when receiving feedback or continued failure to take ownership of actions and decisions
- Deterioration in the relationship with you or other colleagues
- Unprofessional classroom behavior, such as the use of inappropriate language or leaving students unattended
- Persistent lapses of professional responsibilities that affect students, such as arriving to school late, missing or incomplete lesson plans, or lack of responsiveness to important messages or emails
- Lack of change after several debriefs on the same issue

- Trends in beliefs or behaviors that aren't vocalized
- Behavior or beliefs that jeopardize the teacher's job

Preparation

As the great American musician Bo Diddly sang, "Before you accuse me, take a look at yourself." First take time to reflect on whether you might have a mindset of your own about this teacher.

Does a personality conflict predispose you to be overly critical? Are you subconsciously thinking, "This teacher…" when you may need to make an adjustment in your coaching? Do you consistently uphold the value or practice you plan to address during the mindset conversation? For example, do you consistently address answering emails in a timely fashion across all teachers, or are you only addressing this person? In these instances, take time to improve your own approach to the teacher rather than having a conversation with them directly.

Sometimes another administrator or instructional leader will come to you about an incident or overheard comment. In that case, you would investigate to uncover the full story, and then coach them on how to pursue a conversation with the teacher or facilitate the conversation yourself.

Schedule time with a trusted colleague to plan and role play the conversation. Think about how the teacher might react, what might derail the conversation, and plan around it. As you prepare for the conversation, you can use the structure below to guide your planning:

1. Name the problem you're experiencing clearly and directly.
2. Describe the unintended consequences that are occurring for you, the teacher's colleagues, or their students.
3. Identify the ideal outcome that you would like to see happen.
4. Invite a response, and work with the teacher to reach the ideal outcome.

Implementation

Before you go into the meeting, it might help to re-read chapter 2 on "Building Teacher Relationships." It is important to keep at the forefront of your mind that this is not an adversarial relationship. A mindset conversation can be perceived as an attack, and that's exactly what you want to avoid. You must take every precaution to begin with and maintain an attitude of openness and concern and to avoid any hint of judgment. At the outset, and throughout the conversation, seek to understand the teacher's perspective.

You also need to be direct so that your teacher understands what you are talking about and what is at stake. Refer to the Instructional Coaching Excellence Rubric in Chapter 1, particularly the section on direct tone and language. Discomfort, which is a natural response to conflict, can lead you to avoid addressing the issue by making vague statements. If you're not clear, the conversation will not have the desired effect on teacher behavior. It is important that the teacher understands what will happen if the situation doesn't improve and hears what you would like to happen instead.

This is where data can come to your aid. Rather than make assertions, use evidence-impact statements and low-inference data points to illustrate the problem from an objective perspective. Drill down to root causes by pressing the teacher to elaborate. You might ask what experiences led to their current perspective or how they are feeling about the situation.

Recognize that, even though you have taken great pains to plan this conversation, ultimately it can't be scripted; you must be present and aware, and adapt as the situation requires. For example, if emotions run high, step back to break the momentum and say, "I'm sensing some tension. Tell me what's going on in your mind right now."

Silence is often overlooked as a valuable technique in this type of conversation. Allow space for the teacher to process the information and reflect. Resist the urge to fill an uncomfortable silence.

In some cases, part of the problem may stem from an unaddressed need relating to another adult, like a planning partner or campus administrator. In this case, you can help the teacher advocate for themselves by guiding them in the art of directly addressing issues with the person in question. For example:

- A planning partner may send lesson plans to the teacher at the last minute, making preparation and practice impossible. Or, the partner may send lesson plans that lack sufficient detail, requiring extra work for the teacher to make them usable.
- The teacher may think that an evaluator's ratings are unfair.
- In a shared-classroom situation, the previous teacher may be keeping students over, leaving your teacher with little time to transition and prepare the room.

The mindset conversation is important because even the best coaching on knowledge and skill can be derailed by an ingrained attitude or belief. It may take more than one conversation to fully address a mindset issue, so you must bring commitment and persistence to the table. As the chapter "Building Teacher Relationships" points out, teachers are more receptive to mindset conversations when you have taken the pains to build a strong relationship. In fact, a mindset conversation can serve to strengthen the relationship when teachers realize you are willing to be real with them and call out issues that lie below the surface.

Real-time Coaching

In a real-time coaching touchpoint, you use cues, signals, cards, or even a microphone/earpiece to communicate specific teacher moves to the novice teacher with minimum disruption to the lesson, much like a soccer coach on the sidelines prompts players to execute a specific action discussed earlier during practice. The goal is to give teachers feedback in the moment that they can implement immediately to see the impact on the class. This will lead to immediate practice of the skill, which will in turn mean more buy-in from the teacher when they see it work, and ideally more consistent implementation when the coach is not in the room.

To get the most impact out of real-time coaching, we recommend that you use this strategy as a series of two to three consecutive coaching interactions. This series of real-time coaching touchpoints will help the teacher see their incremental progress and provide an opportunity for you to coach them on more nuanced feedback. The series structure also provides an accountability system to ensure that the teacher is consistently implementing your feedback, and that you are consistently present to provide support.

Real-time coaching can be effective for a range of teacher needs, from complex or difficult behavior management concerns to more developed teachers needing to refine instructional techniques such as questioning strategies. It is worth noting that this is not a strategy meant to be used for every teacher you support. It is often used when a teacher needs to build a habit of greater classroom awareness. We have identified some scenarios in our own program where real-time coaching is most commonly offered. One scenario is where the teacher is underperforming in basic classroom skills and is highly motivated to improve, but has been inconsistent or totally unable to implement feedback from a previous debrief. For example, you have had your teacher practice redirecting students and you know they possess this skill, however, in class they are overlooking disruptive behavior because they don't see it happening in the first place. Real-time coaching can also work well when a teacher is unable to manage their classroom when multiple issues arise simultaneously (i.e. two students are arguing, another is out of their seat, and someone else is asking them to sign a bathroom pass). Instructionally, real-time coaching touchpoints work well with teachers who have difficulty with in-the-moment teacher moves such as scaffolding whole-class questions from easiest to more difficult, facilitating student dialogue, or giving specific feedback to students on their work during class.

Before the observation

The two primary parts of this touchpoint are the pre-lesson meeting, and then the subsequent real-time coaching during a lesson. Use this touchpoint to develop a key lever you have identified in earlier touchpoints. Plan the lesson, or a specific part of the lesson, with a focus on a specific criterion for success. Work out a limited number of phrases or cues you will use to communicate a change as the lesson progresses. When first starting out, try for just one to three cues until the coach and teacher both build the skill of implementing real-time coaching. If you use an earpiece, have the teacher practice until they're comfortable with recognizing and implementing the cues before they attempt it in front of students.

It is also important to not have a teacher feel embarrassed when starting real-time coaching. It should be a means to build the coaching relationship and get the teacher more invested rather than make them feel bad for needing this extra level of support. During this pre-meeting, make sure you take the time to discuss the teacher's feelings about this process, and potentially script out the message you (or the teacher) will share with students in the class.

During the observation

Give in-the-moment cues to change the teacher's behavior based on the key lever and criteria for success. Take notes of the cue, when it was given, the teacher response, and how it affected students. Note when a teacher did not act on a cue so you can follow up in the debrief. Often this follow up can reveal mindsets that serve as barriers. The template below can be used to take notes during real-time coaching.

Prompts:	With Prompt	Without Prompt
Narration		
Redirection		
Consequence		
Circulation		
Statement		
Restate expectation/ wait for 100%		

After the observation

Once your coaching session has concluded, send the teacher the data from your notes gathered during the observation. Ask the teacher about their take-aways from the experience, and make sure they felt the connection between their actions and the impact on students. Prepare reflection questions and provide your own written feedback. You should customize your reflection questions to align to your own coaching style and the needs of your teacher. Here are some example questions that our coaches ask in real-time-coaching reflections:

- What are your biggest take-aways from the real-time coaching session?
- Was this real-time coaching session effective for you? Why?
- What necessary steps do you still need support to implement monitoring behavior consistently?
- Would you want to participate in more cycles of real-time coaching?

Email your teacher the reflection questions and wait for them to respond before sharing your own glows and grows with them. It sometimes happens that the teacher's reflection does not align with your own, and when this is the case, an additional meeting may be necessary. For example, if in their reflection the teacher notes "I caught every off-task behavior and kids were really well behaved" when in fact they didn't respond to four prompts, there are still existing issues with behavior, and you've identified missed opportunities to implement key teacher moves that you've worked on. The purpose of this meeting is to directly discuss times when the teacher failed to act on a cue to uncover mindset issues around why their perception of class indicates a lack of awareness. Your discussion of feedback from one real-time coaching session can also be a part of the pre-meeting for the next round.

Classroom Reset

The classroom reset is focused on more severe student behavior and management issues. After careful planning and preparation, the teacher devotes an entire class period to engaging the students to clarify expectations, introduce new routines or systems, provide accountability for student behavior, and have students process new rules or practice new routines. Classroom resets are used only when typical coaching conversations about management strategies have been implemented, and it seems unlikely that the situation is going to improve. In such cases, the students and the teacher need a fresh start.

This touchpoint is essential in a situation where the teacher is struggling with managing one or more classes, perhaps due to inconsistent application of expectations, redirections and consequences. In a reset, the novice teacher communicates the rationale for taking a class period to address the problem, establishes that the problem is the result of a lapse on both sides (the teacher hasn't been consistent, the students have not been meeting expectations), and outlines the plan for change.

When the environment in a classroom has reached the point of requiring a reset touchpoint, other stakeholders will likely already be involved. If not, bring them into the loop and have appropriate stakeholders in the classroom during the reset when possible. Supplemental personnel could include the campus administrator who handles student discipline for that grade level, the school counselor, or perhaps a grade-level chair.

The planning session for a reset is much like planning a lesson—you may not be able to plan every aspect of the reset, so it is important to prioritize the facets of the reset that provide the greatest benefit. When you recommend a reset to the teacher, have your rationale prepared. In the case where the novice teacher is aware of the need for change, perhaps having already asked for help, buy-in won't be a problem. If the teacher is unaware of the problem or has been resistant to suggestions during debriefs, you must have the data on hand to establish the need for change and gain buy-in.

Once you have buy-in, move to strengths the teacher has already mastered that can be used in the reset period, and outline a clear process for the reset, such as rationale, non-negotiables, and accountability. Plan the agenda together, model the execution, and then allow the teacher to practice. If the class has students who are especially intractable, you may need to roleplay student objections and responses.

Make sure the novice teacher understands that the key to success is following through with consistency and accountability. Then model that principle in subsequent debriefs with the teacher, consistently holding them accountable for mastering management in the classroom.

Research Integration

In the twenty-first century, those who come to the field of education have taken various routes. Some may have an education degree. Some may come from an expertise in a specific content domain, but have no prior experience working with children. Some may be leaving a career in an unrelated field to become classroom teachers. Regardless of their path, even experienced teachers can benefit from new findings in the field. A research touchpoint provides a path for the novice teacher to learn new moves based on modern research into best classroom practices.

This touchpoint is especially suited for novice teachers with a learning style geared for reading and reflecting, particularly those seeking a wider validation beyond the experience of a single individual. In other words, if a teacher sometimes has difficulty taking your word that a strategy will work, research articles lend an outside perspective and credence. Coaching with research articles has the added benefit of building a skill that can sustain the novice teacher in future years when individual coaching is no longer available. Those who learn how to learn will never be at a loss for exploring new ways of taking their practice to the next level.

A novice teacher may express a need for development in a specific area. You must weigh their perceived need against your judgment of the actual gaps in effectiveness in the classroom and direct the novice teacher toward the key lever that will have the greatest impact on student achievement. For example, a teacher struggling with classroom management should not be spending time researching fun activities. A research touchpoint works best for teachers performing at the average or above average level, and who may also be able to handle multiple areas of focus.

Selecting the article

If you determine that a research touchpoint is the best option, start by selecting appropriate articles from peer-reviewed academic journals. While the process outlined below may feel time-intensive or tedious, once you've found an article that is appropriate, you will likely reuse this same article with other teachers in the future. You can use a few tricks that to streamline the process. We recommend selecting a user-friendly academic search engine that enables you to quickly sift through articles based on your parameters. If you have a specific article in mind but are having trouble locating a copy, consider checking with your local library, or reach out to a local university to assist you with your search. Often an author of an article can be reached via email directly. Search for articles that are no more than 10 years old to help ensure that the practices you are discussing are timely and up-to-date.

When determining which articles will best suit your needs, read through the abstract, which will typically outline the object of the study, the types of students and classrooms studied (elementary or middle school, low-income or middle-income students, etc.) and the results. A research touchpoint must be based in academic research from a peer-reviewed journal. Avoid blogs, news articles, op-ed columns, and the like. You want research-based principles, not conjecture.

After you've identified the right article for your teacher, your next step is to process the article by reading it in full. As you read, highlight specific portions of the article that you want the teacher to read, omitting information that feels superfluous or tangential to your discussion. It is not typically necessary for the teacher to read the methods section for example, so most of your highlighting will be in the introduction, results, and discussion sections of the article. This will save your teacher the time required to pour through pages of content to parse out what's important. After you've read and highlighted, develop three to six key points that frame the focus of your debrief with the teacher.

Once the article is processed, send it to your teacher about week in advance of the meeting; this will respect their time and give them ample opportunity to read the selection thoroughly for comprehension, rather than skimming through it. Have the teacher complete a reflection on the reading. Generally, you want to know how much the teacher already knows about the topic, what their general impressions were while reading, and if they have any initial ideas for implementing the strategy or replicating the outcomes of the study. Some example questions or prompts that our coaches ask teachers are:

- Before you read this article, can you briefly summarize your existing knowledge of this topic? Read the abstract for a specific context if necessary.
- What were your general take-aways from reading the article?
- Do you have any initial ideas for implementation in your class?
- What are some potential barriers you foresee?
- What remaining questions do you have about the article?

It is crucial that the teacher read the article and do the reflection before coming to the debrief.

Debriefing the article

The process for a research touchpoint conversation is straightforward:

1. Discuss the key points.
2. Discuss initial ideas.
3. Refine strategy
4. Plan or practice

At the beginning of the debrief, compare the key points you created with the teacher's take-aways to ensure you are aligned on the key points. Having them already written down enables you to quickly share a key point that a teacher may have overlooked or didn't consider significant. You can open the dialogue by asking, "What were your take-aways from the article?" or "What stood out to you as most important as you read this?"

Once you have established that you're aligned, discuss the teacher's initial ideas, which should be recorded in the reflection document. For example, if the article is on project-based-learning, the teacher may already have a specific project in mind. If the article focused on managing peer-peer interactions in a middle school classroom, the teacher may have a specific group of students or a class period that they are most concerned with. The critical component here is to create a space for the teacher to have agency on implementation strategies. It's okay if you have a clearer vision for the outcome than the teacher does. It's still important to give them the opportunity to express their ideas while also being ready to provide the necessary guidance and perspective.

Once you have agreed on implementation, revisit the key points from the article and use them to refine the strategy. For example, for project-based learning, the article may suggest two or three scaffolds for PBL implementation. Some of these suggested scaffolds may be more relevant or more accessible than others for the project the teacher has in mind. During this portion of the debrief, your goal is to identify those components of the research that are most reasonable for the teacher to implement given the context of their classroom and personal experience.

Spend the rest of the debrief planning or practicing the research-based knowledge or skills. This should be a collaborative effort with the teacher doing most of the heavy lifting. Your role as the teacher educator is to provide strategic guidance using the recommendations from the article and your own experience.

A final point to remember with research touchpoints is that research articles themselves are not prescriptive. Devising specific action steps for implementation may require some level of collaborative interpretation between you and your teacher.

The reflective practitioner touchpoint is best suited for an experienced coach working with a high-functioning teacher with high skill and high will. It allows the coach and teacher to examine a data set and derive next steps using the Socratic method. It is less directive and more exploratory than a traditional touchpoint and can help the teacher develop the skill to diagnose issues and find solutions independently. It has the added advantage of demonstrating the degree of trust you have in the teacher, allowing them to own their forward progress.

This touchpoint moves you and the teacher into a collaborative, partnership approach, transitioning the teacher to a peer-based relationship. You and the teacher begin by looking at a common set of data such as a classroom observation, using questions and teacher input to drive the debrief. Possible questions include:

- What do you want your ideal student discussion to look like?
- How did today's discussion meet that ideal?
- How did today's discussion not meet that ideal?
- How can we push it toward the ideal?

Once you and the teacher have identified a focus, collaboratively generate solutions. Based on your experience, you can offer your own theories about the data and propose possible solutions. Eventually you should converge on an agreed solution and then model and practice the strategy.

Flexibility is a core skill that teacher educators must possess to be the resource that their teachers need. The best advice for any teacher hoping to differentiate for their students is to know their audience. The same applies to teacher educators. By simultaneously seeking to understand the method through which each teacher you support learns best and cultivating the practice of analyzing each key lever for the appropriate touchpoint, you'll find that in time you will more consistently make the appropriate developmental choice in your coaching and more regularly increase the impact of the change you seek.

Two specific types of alternate touchpoints are used enough by our teacher educators to warrant more in-depth discussion in the next two chapters. They are the touchpoints that center around coaching on two of the most crucial skills for new teachers to become proficient at: lesson planning and the use of data.

1. Do the following as a planning exercise: Make a list of the teachers you support, and identify at least one alternative coaching touchpoint that you think would be most impactful for them presently.

2. Of all the various structures for coaching interactions discussed in this chapter, which strategies are you already most comfortable with? Which strategies have you not tried, or are the least familiar with? Of the latter, which will you prioritize becoming more familiar with as a coaching tool?

3. Alternate touchpoints can be an opportunity to collaborate. Who is someone (e.g. a district or content specialist, or experienced campus teacher) you could ask to conduct a focus lesson for one of your teachers? Who is a teacher who would be a good example for a co-observation?

12

Lesson Planning Touchpoints

"It is better to look ahead and prepare than to look back and regret."

— Jackie Joyner-Kersee

Imagine a teacher whose key lever is in their ability to effectively create a lesson plan. This is not an atypical struggle for novice teachers to wrestle with at one time or another, and perhaps you have coached teachers like this in the past. Imagine, further, that this teacher's coach only employs the traditional observation-debrief touchpoint with them throughout their first year. Each time they meet to debrief, the gap they identify is a symptom of this root cause of ineffective planning. Perhaps one week, the key lever revolves around the delivery of a clear teacher-model to students, and another touchpoint focuses on questioning students in a way that encourages all students to engage. Even though each of these skills are valuable and these touchpoints result in some change, the classroom never makes the jump that would be expected if things really "clicked" for that teacher. If, after two to three such touchpoints, this teacher's coach was to hypothesize that all these symptoms have a common key lever in planning, that coach would be wise to implement a lesson planning touchpoint and address the issue at the source in a way that could set this teacher up to close all these gaps on a regular basis.

A lesson planning touchpoint involves two key steps and flips the order of a typical observation and debrief:

1. Plan part of a lesson with a teacher during a meeting.
2. Observe the teacher present the lesson and provide written (glow and grow) feedback.

For example, you and the teacher would first plan an engaging student practice activity, then you would observe that portion of the lesson within the next two days after the meeting. After the observation, you would leave the teacher written feedback on how their planning paid off for students and areas where they can continue to improve the lesson. Point out the positive impact of lesson planning skills on student outcomes and opportunities for continued improvement that arise during the observation.

Because this type of touchpoint reverses the order of the observation and the meeting, we call it a "reverse touchpoint."

Pro-Tip: Because the order is reversed, lesson planning touchpoints can be tricky to schedule with a teacher. Give yourself extra time to get these meetings on your calendar, placing the debrief before the observation.

Identifying the Need

There are several scenarios that can be addressed with a lesson planning touchpoint. Novice teachers all need support with lesson planning, but they don't all need the support for the same reason, and thus, their specific issues must be addressed differently.

Planning takes too long

Planning lessons is taking an inordinate amount of time, affecting the teacher's personal life and possibly costing them sleep. As a result, their lesson execution suffers. This struggle is especially common among first-year teachers and can adversely affect retention, as it is often self-reported as a cause why people fail to return to the profession.

Lesson plans are absent

The teacher isn't submitting lesson plans. They may be planning on the same day as the class or may not be planning at all and instead are just winging it in class.

Lesson plans are not being internalized

When teachers are provided with lesson plans or required to use a scripted curriculum, sometimes they do not take the time to internalize and modify the plans to meet the needs of their specific students.

Lesson plans are incomplete

The teacher isn't planning with sufficient detail or is glossing over certain components, leading to problems with execution in the classroom that affect student achievement. You may be able to isolate the planning components that are weak and address them individually. If the teacher's performance or the students' understanding consistently breaks down at a certain point in the lesson, you can focus planning on that component.

Teacher performance is inconsistent

During observations, you have identified gaps in the teacher's performance, but are unsure if they are due to planning or execution. For example, if you have previously coached the teacher to verify that they're monitoring students during group or individual practice, but the practice part of their lesson is still weak, a lesson planning touchpoint may be in order.

Students are struggling

If a certain group of students consistently struggles in class, you can take the opportunity to focus on differentiation when planning lessons. For example, you can focus on differentiating the lesson for English language learners, students with special needs, high-achieving students, or any other subgroup.

A major evaluation is imminent

When a teacher is scheduled for a major evaluation, you might want to plan together to ensure that they are prepared for the evaluation. Depending on the need, lesson planning touchpoints can take just 45 minutes for a specific skill or can be given more time for larger topics.

Planning the Conversation

First, determine the goal of the touchpoint based on the gap you are seeking to close and the amount of time you have for the conversation. The key lever must improve student performance in the classroom and involve a transferable skill that can be covered within the available time.

Schedule the date and time of the meeting with the teacher, indicating that you will be collaborating on creating a lesson plan. Establish the pre-work that the teacher should bring to the meeting, which will allow the two of you to focus your energies on the component of the lesson planning process that will close the gap. For example, if a teacher's focus is questioning, starting with a blank document will waste everyone's time. In this case, the teacher should come to the meeting with a complete lesson plan, or at least a vision for a portion of an upcoming lesson.

Pro-Tip: Plan the meeting far enough in advance for the teacher to reasonably accomplish all pre-work in addition to their other duties.

Remember that the goal of the touchpoint is to outline, model, and have the teacher practice a reproducible process that will strengthen the teacher's ability to plan lessons on their own. Just as in a standard coaching conversation, your criteria for success are the driver of a lesson planning debrief as well. Break the focus skill down into digestible steps that can be used in many situations. If you have trouble identifying the steps, think through a couple of lessons you have developed and generalize the steps into a template or process.

If there are staff members on your campus who do this skill exceedingly well, reach out to them as a resource. Gather their lesson plans in advance to show your teacher what it looks like to think through this skill in such a way that it supports strong lesson execution.

If you (or your teacher) don't have content expertise in the lesson under construction, bring textbooks, long-term plans, or other aids. If you do have content expertise, your own lesson plans and resources can provide a starting point, allowing you go through your own thought process with a level of detail that would be impossible if you were to borrow the plans of another teacher on your campus.

To model the planning of a lesson, write the plan or part of the plan in advance, but during the meeting work from a blank lesson plan form so the teacher can see your process live and in the moment as you make decisions.

Executing the Conversation

As always, start the meeting off with relationship building and then segue into the evidence that lead you to this focus area. You have likely already talked to the teacher about planning together. Clearly name the skill you will develop and provide a bird's-eye view of the process. Then, using your personal exemplars or the exemplars you gathered, show each step in developing the lesson plan and model the thought process that goes into the skill. Be as explicit as possible. You may want to highlight things the exemplar doesn't have or didn't do to point out common pitfalls.

Next, on the teacher's lesson plan, execute the steps together. As you proceed, the teacher will naturally focus on the specifics of the lesson. Affirm the application to this lesson while pointing out the general step they are executing and how it applies to the development of any lesson plan, not just this one.

As you wrap up the meeting, bring the focus back to the evidence you gathered while observing the classroom. Invite the teacher to consider the impact executing these steps during planning would have had on the class. What will change in their class as they regularly use this skill? As usual, tie everything back to student outcomes: "If this change occurs, then the number of students who master tomorrow's objective should increase from the 60% mastery we saw in today's class."

In closing, give the teacher any next steps that are needed to complete the lesson plan or prepare to execute the lesson.

Observing the Results

As you observe the teacher deliver the lesson, look for the elements that were covered during the lesson planning touchpoint and limit your written feedback to those details. Ask the teacher to reflect on any differences they saw in the classroom and to send you a new lesson plan that they created independently. In future debriefs and meetings, look for opportunities to note growth that is related to lesson planning to keep the ball moving, to ensure clarity on the part of the teacher and to follow-through in building the habit.

136

Planning a lesson is a long and detailed process when you stop to consider all that is required. In a lesson planning debrief, you want to focus on just one change the teacher can make. Below are some of the specific focus areas we have found helpful for new teachers.

Scope and Sequence

This type of lesson planning touchpoint focuses on the high-level planning exercise of deriving a weekly scope-and-sequence from an existing unit plan. The product is not a set of fully fleshed out daily plans, but rather a skeleton that indicates the shape that the instruction for a week will take. The deliverable is a set of objectives, key points, and resources for each day of instruction. The teacher then uses the scope and sequence to generate detailed lesson plans.

The source document for this type of planning is usually a unit plan from a district or campus curriculum development team or perhaps curriculum purchased from an educational materials provider. Statewide standards can also serve as a source document for planning. Using these documents can help a teacher who is planning day-to-day, or who has a weak understanding of how objectives are connected.

During the meeting, guide the teacher through the scope-and-sequence development process using generalized steps that aren't dependent on the content of the lesson. When the deliverable is complete, articulate specific action steps the teacher should take to identify the skill to model for each lesson and finalize the lesson plan by a specific deadline.

Specific Section

Use this lesson planning touchpoint type to focus on a specific section of the lesson plan or a specific move within the lesson. There are several ways to segment the lesson plan. Select one element within a structure and guide the teacher through the process of developing the element using generalized steps that aren't dependent on the content. Choose only one section to focus on based on the gap you're observing in the classroom.

Traditional Lesson Plan Elements	
Introduction to new material	Introduce or explain the objective and the key points
Teacher model	Think aloud or model the skill that students will master
Checks for understanding	Questions incorporated into the lesson to ensure students understand the key points
Guided practice	Practice activities that align to the objective and allow the students to practice with their peers and with feedback from the teacher
Independent practice	Practice activities that align to the objective and allow students to practice on their own
Exit ticket	Assessment delivered at the end of a lesson that demonstrates student learning; must be aligned to the objective and appropriately rigorous

The Five Es	
Engage	Teacher hooks the students' interest in the topic
Explore	Teacher provides students an opportunity to build on their background knowledge
Explain	Teacher clarifies definitions, key points, and processes
Elaborate	Students complete a more in-depth practice
Evaluate	Students demonstrate their learning

PDP sections	
Pre-Reading	Teacher introduces the objective and key points, models the skill, gives a quick review of the story, and defines any vocabulary needed
During Reading	Teacher and students practice the skill together using a text
Post-Reading	Students demonstrate their comprehension independently

Menu Planning

This type of lesson planning touchpoint creates a list of several ideas for each element in the lesson plan. The teacher can then select an idea from each element as if the lesson is a three- to five-course meal, depending on the number of elements in the lesson plan.

For example, using a traditional lesson plan structure, you and the teacher would brainstorm several ideas for introducing new material, several ideas for modeling the skill, and so on. You should prepare several ideas for each category ahead of time, but push the teacher to contribute as many ideas as possible before offering your suggestions.

Pro-Tip: Use a timer to keep on course. The brainstorming shouldn't consume the bulk of the meeting. The goal is to push the most immediate thoughts out onto the planning document.

For example, one high-flying first-year teacher with an undergraduate degree in education arrived at a meeting on the brink of tears because lesson planning was eating into personal time for her family on the weekend. Because she had strong teacher moves to push through any lesson, the coach suggested they brainstorm a bank of ideas for each stage of her five-step lessons. The session jump-started the teacher's planning and she was able to more efficiently plan her lessons in the available time at school.

Backward Planning

This type of lesson planning touchpoint uses the principle of understanding by design (UbD) to analyze the desired outcome and then design the lesson plan to achieve the outcome. The starting point can be a weekly quiz, an exit ticket, or a unit exam.

This is a good approach to use with a teacher who has a lot of content knowledge, but has trouble distilling the knowledge into digestible chunks for instruction and evaluation. For example, a physics graduate may struggle with parsing their extensive understanding of thermodynamics into the essential elements required to transfer the appropriate level of understanding to an eleventh-grade class. In this case, the meeting starts with creating a ten-question weekly quiz or a three-question exit ticket to help narrow the focus and ensure alignment. With the quiz or exit ticket as a source document, guide the teacher through the steps of extrapolating the target requirements into teachable chunks for each day.

Pro-Tip: While this is a type of lesson planning on its own, it's important to note that internal alignment (achieved through backwards planning) should be emphasized in any type of lesson planning meeting. This can be a difficult skill for novice teachers, so the coach should explicitly reference how a specific section of the lesson or a specific idea within a menu will lead to an aligned lesson.

Truly, there are no exemplary teachers without exemplary plans. Certainly, there are teachers whose ability to read their students apprehension or to problem solve on the fly may allow them to get more out of a plan than someone else. However, for teachers to grow in the profession of education, their ability to plan provides both the floor and the ceiling for their current ability. As their planning ability rises, so too does the floor for a bad day, and the ceiling for an average or outstanding day with their students. Even the best teachers can benefit from the occasional step-back to analyze and improve their regular planning process and this is even more necessary for the novice teacher, as they work to find their place in this incredibly demanding and infinitely rewarding profession.

~ CHAPTER REFLECTION ~

1. Go to the "Areas of Focus" section of this chapter. Categorize some of your teachers based on each approach to lesson planning and which style might best fit their current needs.

2. What is a specific campus or district instructional initiative that you are implementing this year? Plan a lesson-planning touchpoint with your novice teachers about how you would like them to support this initiative. Write a criteria for success outlining what good implementation looks like in their classroom.

3. Who is a campus or district stakeholder that you could recruit to help support specific lesson planning skills for your teachers?

13

CHAPTER 13 **Data-Driven Coaching**

Using student achievement data to adjust instruction is a skill that can help teachers continually improve over the entirety of their career. For novice teachers, data analysis can be very tricky because it encompasses a subset of nuanced skills: knowing how to routinely collect student data, how to identify trends and draw appropriate conclusions, and how to use that information to inform instruction. Each of these skills requires varying degrees of guidance and support depending on a teacher's need. For this reason, TE emphasizes the practice of *student achievement data integration*, a coaching technique whereby students' academic data is woven into the majority of coaching conversations. This data then gradually inculcates the habit of reflecting on what students have accomplished and allows teachers to adjust future instruction accordingly.

Another common practice is to conduct a *data dive*. A data dive is a single-event coaching conversation where the teacher educator and novice teacher sit down to analyze and action plan around a large set of summative assessment data, often the results of district or state benchmark exams. Data dives will be discussed in the second half of this chapter, though we do recommend that teacher educators prioritize *student achievement data integration* over conducting *data dives* with first-year teachers.

Many first-year teachers are planning day-to-day or week-to-week, which makes it difficult for them to envision long-term academic adjustments. Additionally, many of the needs of a novice teacher are more immediate—needing to reteach yesterday's lesson because students were still confused, or needing to give students additional practice time for the current focus skill. For these reasons, data integration for first-year teachers is best done on a regular basis with smaller data sets: looking at student answers from independent practice in a lesson, exit tickets from a single lesson, quiz data for that week, or unit exam data from the most recent grading period. In short, analyzing daily, weekly, or unit data generates more developmentally appropriate action items that match first-year teachers' work flow.

Student Achievement Data Integration			
Not Meeting Expectations	**Approaching Proficiency**	**Proficient**	**Mastery**
• The coach misses an opportunity to introduce student achievement data based on key lever	• There is evidence which demonstrates the coach has planned a general approach to discussing data with the teacher • There is a missed opportunity to collaboratively analyze student data to inform action planning or the data analysis is driven entirely by the coach • There is no evidence of a data-centered goal for the teacher's classroom	• There is evidence which demonstrates the coach has specifically planned with the teacher's developmental and/or student achievement data context in mind • Coach and teacher collaboratively analyze student data to inform action planning • There is evidence of a data-centered goal for the teacher's classroom that is referenced as part of the debrief or as an element of follow-up	• There is evidence which demonstrates the coach has consistently and strategically planned with the teacher's developmental and student achievement data context in mind in order to target strategic and specific gaps • Coach and teacher collaboratively analyze class and individual student level performance or sub-population performance • There is evidence of a data-centered goal for the teacher's classroom that is referenced and used set benchmarks and progress monitor towards the goal

Analyzing student achievement data as a specific coaching practice is represented in the ICER as its own indicator. To summarize, the teacher educator should introduce an appropriate data set during their coaching conversation and then collaborate with the teacher to analyze that data and determine how the teacher should proceed with adjusting instruction for the next or future lessons. While there are several strategies for accomplishing this as a coach (discussed below), note that the mastery language for "student achievement data integration" on the ICER indicates that ultimately the goal is to guide the teacher toward more focused decisions and specific interventions for individual students or specific sub-populations. Early in a coaching relationship, you will likely be more directive with data integration—selecting the data and telling a teacher what to do when you've identified a common trend in their class(es). As your teachers develop their craft and expand their pedagogical toolkits, adjust your approach to give teachers more opportunities to voice their ideas before presenting your own. This way, by the end their first school year, your teacher is equipped with the knowledge and skills to do this work on their own as they enter year two and beyond.

Whether at the beginning of the school year or toward the end, teacher educators generally incorporate student data when discussing a teacher's strengths and areas for growth. This not only gives teachers an opportunity for input when they hear feedback, it also better grounds your feedback in the people who matter most: students. Once you get to application and practice, teachers are generally more invested in the change that they need to make.

What data to integrate

Student achievement data should be introduced relative to the key lever identified during your classroom observation. It is also important to note that data integration may not be strategic, or even possible, at the beginning of the school year because of the developmental trajectory of novice teachers.

Suppose, for example, you support a science teacher who is struggling to establish basic routines for lab days: Students don't have quick access to materials, the procedures are confusing, and, in many groups, only one or two students are attempting the work in earnest while others are distracted. Because of this struggle, students are frequently not completing the investigation and follow-up work. The key lever here (routines for lab days and group work) stands on its own evidence; sitting down with the teacher to comb through a stack of incomplete lab reports belabors the point in a non-productive way and could negatively impact the teacher's motivation. In this type of early-year situation, you should still strive to use *observational* data and/or *student-outcome* data to craft your evidence impact statements (see Chapter 5, "Observing the Classroom") to highlight the urgent need for a more thorough lab-day plan.

True data integration comes into play when *student achievement* data is introduced into the debrief. You should begin data integration when your coaching shifts from behavioral/classroom culture key levers to instructional key levers.

Discussed below are several examples of student achievement data to integrate into your debriefs and strategies for leveraging them.

Classroom Work

As previously discussed, there are many methods to capture samples of student work: collecting the work itself after class (either you or the teacher can do this), taking pictures of what students produced, capturing video of student interactions, etc. Whatever your method, analyzing the results of student work for a particular lesson is a great starting place for teachers to learn how to identify common misunderstandings, concepts which need to be retaught, or by contrast, which concepts students understood or mastered.

Until your teacher develops a habit of consistently analyzing student performance on daily tasks or assignments, you will need to identify what aspect of a particular

143

assignment that you want to focus on before the debrief. In other words, if questions 7-10 on a 10-question assignment are the most important in terms of measuring student success on the day's objective, then you should not plan to discuss the first six questions in depth, if at all. Think about the assignment and subsequent student performance from both a qualitative and a quantitative standpoint. Where do students demonstrate a trend in mastery or misunderstanding? How many students met expectations and how many did not? Look at what students were tasked with and identify for yourself what critical questions to ask. The answer to those questions will inform how you and your teacher proceed.

In an effort to cultivate this type of reflective practice in your teachers, prompt them with initial reflection questions that mirror the same thought process you use. Ask teachers questions: What would an ideal answer sound like? Who provided an answer like this? Who came close, and who missed the mark entirely? As you prompt your teacher with these questions, be transparent about what you're doing. In effect, you may need a guided-questions-style criteria-for-success to teach them the right questions to ask themselves as they consider data.

However the class work is analyzed, remember that action steps resulting from student work analysis should be developmentally appropriate for the teacher—i.e. September (for most novice teachers) may not be the most strategic time to start adjusting the rigor of an assignment.

Exit Tickets

Exit tickets provide an easy and organic vehicle for analyzing student achievement data with teachers once the system for issuing regular exit tickets is in place. Many novice teachers are aware early in the year that exit tickets (or some means of measuring the success of that day's lesson) are an important component of instruction, but they may not have a consistent practice of using them. Think about the trajectory of your teacher's development and know that they may need you to coach them on how to establish a routine of issuing an exit ticket at the end of most lessons, or how to plan for a weekly quiz before you can consistently analyze these for student achievement.

An exit ticket sort can be done either before or after an observation, and is a speedy way to analyze data for multiple classes of students.

The teacher needs to bring graded exit tickets to the meeting. Sort the exit tickets into two or three piles, working with the teacher to determine the score that you would use to sort assessments. For example, the teacher might tell you that their goal is 80 percent mastery, so then you make two piles—those above 80 percent and those below. If the teacher hasn't identified what their mastery threshold is, make three piles: students who scored between 80-100 percent (mastery), students who scored between 60-80 percent (approaching mastery), and students who scored below a 60 percent (not yet mastered). Depending on the mastery level in the individual lesson, you may need to adjust these cut scores.

Once you have piles, look more closely at each pile to look for trends. What is the major difference between the students who did well and the students who didn't? Did students all make the same error? Did they miss the same question or set of questions? Were the questions actually aligned with what was taught?

Once you've identified trends, there are a variety of possible action steps available ranging from minor course corrections to major adjustments. Perhaps your teacher needs to simply clarify an explanation or an example discussed in class, or they may need to re-teach the entire objective the next day, or pull the students who did poorly for a small group tutorial. Whatever the case may be, use your own pedagogical toolkit to point your teacher in the right direction and to coach them through a successful follow-up with their students.

Weekly Quizzes

Analyzing data from a weekly quiz gives a teacher a clear vision for any instructional changes they need to make for the week ahead. Similar to exit tickets, it may be necessary to coach your teacher first on establishing the instructional routine of quizzing students on a weekly basis. Once they have met this benchmark, collaboratively looking at that student data can also become a regular part of your coaching conversations.

A common practice is once again to sort the quiz results into three or four categories of student proficiency. The number of students in each pile will inform the level of intervention necessary. If only a few students are below proficiency, then a small group explanation with those students may be all that is needed. If a larger portion of the class did not demonstrate sufficient understanding, the teacher may need to reteach the concept entirely, or conduct a mini-lesson on a specific common misunderstanding.

It is also a common recommendation that the teacher present the most frequently missed questions on a future quiz to ensure that their intervention was indeed effective and that students did indeed comprehend the material.

Data for Non-Traditional Subjects

For courses in which students do not take regular paper-pencil assessments, teachers still need to develop the skill of using data, but may approach it in a different way. One effective coaching action is to work with the teacher to create a rubric for quantifying the quality of student work. The rubric should explain what the best possible product looks like, and then break down what the product would look like at a beginning stage, final stage, and every stage in between.

This works well for electives like art, physical education, or theater, and intervention courses that might exist for core subjects like reading and math. For more qualitative student assignments, the rubric helps you and the teacher assess and improve student achievement. In art classes, teachers can also break down criteria for using a certain style, and assess whether or not students met that criteria.

In physical education, for example, teachers should be setting goals with students and for their class for student fitness and determining how progress toward that goal is measured. For example, teachers may be recording students' mile times on a regular basis and can analyze that data to improve student health and fitness.

For technology courses, rubrics are also helpful here to determine the quality of the work students are producing. You may also help the teacher design a performance task where they observe a student navigating a particular program or achieving a certain task and determine whether the student met their criteria.

Assessments in early childhood are often performance tasks where you observe a student completing the task and then mark whether they did it according to criteria and with ease or fluency. For example, you may observe students counting a number of manipulatives and writing numbers and then mark down how the student is developing his sense of one-to-one correspondence.

Data Dives

Data and Novice Teachers

We strongly recommend that teachers and coaches use student data in every coaching conversation in the ways described above. There may be times during the year, though, that it makes sense for you and a teacher to spend an entire debrief looking at a set of data. We call this a "data dive," and recommend scheduling it like a reverse touchpoint—with the meeting first, followed by an observation of action items driven by the data.

Data dives for first-year teachers are best done more regularly with smaller sets of data—unit exams, for example—rather than a few times a year with larger pieces of data. Most first-year teachers are planning day-to-day and, at best, week-to-week. Analyzing weekly or unit data generates action items that match first-year teachers' work flow. For example, analyzing data from a weekly quiz gives a teacher a change they need to make for the week ahead. Larger pieces of data, like benchmark exams or interim assessments, generate action items that need to be a focus for a few months or an entire semester. One action step generated by benchmark or interim data may be that the teacher needs to hold tutoring sessions for students once a week for the rest of the semester. While this is absolutely possible, it requires that teacher to be constantly aware of both the original data and additional data points to decide who's in the tutorial group. For first-year teachers who may be struggling with more foundational teaching practices, that action item is overwhelming. It's better, then, to focus on more immediate assessments and to generate items more often so that teachers are making regular improvements that will still impact student achievement on larger exams.

While we feel this caveat is true for the majority of our first-year teachers, it is not true for all of them. We coach teachers who are ready to look at larger pieces of data during their first year, and even early in their teaching career. These teachers often use skills from data dives to look at all the data they have access to and request more data analysis help from their coaches. If you feel a teacher is ready to look at benchmark tests or interim assessments, by all means, make that a part of your coaching.

As an administrator, you may interact with larger pieces of data more regularly. Analyzing benchmark exams and interim assessments is often part of your role. You may then report out trends and action items to district staff or to the campus. Many campuses have initiatives, like incorporating literacy strategies across contents, that are based on state testing results or other large assessment data pulls. Many of our campuses analyze data from large assessments together during professional development, which allows novice teachers to get help from administrators or experienced teachers.

Considerations Before a Data Dive

Enter with an open mind

You want the data to speak for itself. Coaches often have predictions about where student scores may be, or have future action items in mind based on the last time they coached. For example, you may have just coached a teacher on improving their introduction of key points, and you know you want to work on questioning next. When coaches have those thoughts top-of-mind during a data dive, they risk misinterpreting data. If possible, it's best to take a look at a teacher's data before the meeting so you have an idea of the trends. It's crucial that you enter a data dive ready to see what the data is telling you and to move your coaching in that direction, even if it deviates somewhat from your original plan.

This can be especially difficult when you are coaching a resistant teacher who is struggling with foundational skills and whose students do extremely well on an assessment. You have likely spent the last few coaching interactions trying to convince this teacher that they really do need to change their teaching practice if they want kids to be successful. Then their data comes back and they may think, "See, coach? My kids did amazing! Best in the district! I don't need to change my teaching at all." In this case, coaches need to give the teacher the opportunity to rise to the occasion. Their students just did great, and probably need advanced teacher skills to keep them on their trajectory of growth. The coach may also need to tell the teacher that these initial student results are likely a combination of what they've done and what the teacher last year did. If the teacher doesn't improve, student achievement will either stagnate or start to decline.

Scheduling

For a data dive, you generally want the meeting to occur before the observation. Get the meeting on the calendar first. Once you analyze the data and create action items, that determines what you need to observe. For example, you may need to come observe after-school tutorials OR you may need to come see how the seating chart is working out in second period. These are very different pieces of time to schedule an observation and can't really be done until the end of your data dive meeting. One piece of advice is to schedule the first component, the meeting, and then schedule a longer hold with the teacher so you know you need to return to their class but you have a larger chunk of time to play with.

Data dive meetings should be no shorter than 45 minutes, but often take longer than a traditional debrief. These meetings sometimes happen during whole-school staff meetings to analyze data, in which case you can use that entire time to work with a teacher who needs developing this skill. It's best to schedule these meetings after school or during a part of the day when you could extend the meeting to an hour.

Resources

You will want the teacher to arrive to the meeting with the data in some form. The pre-work depends on the teacher's level of preparation and what your school or district has access to. Early in the year, teachers may not be familiar with data software, and, therefore, much of that work of pulling the data needs to be done in the meeting. Make sure you account for that when you schedule the meeting, and add 10-15 extra minutes to pull the data.

At any point in the year, you can ask teachers to bring graded assignments, weekly quizzes, or unit assessments. Give the teacher appropriate notice, and let them know that they need to bring all their graded assessments. Depending on the teacher's schedule, they may have data for multiple classes with 30+ students in each class. That's a lot of hard copies to sort through in one meeting. You can choose to analyze all their students, or to analyze just one class period and have them repeat the process for their other classes. Use the tools you have access to and your knowledge of the teacher's development to determine the scope of the analysis.

It's best if the teacher has a tracking system, such as an Excel document or gradebook, where they've already entered this data. That makes the data easy to sort and categorize. If the teacher is consistently using a tracker, have them bring both their hard-copy assessments and the tracker so that you can analyze trends on both a class-level and individual-level. If they're not, creating a tracker will likely be a focus of the meeting.

As the teacher educator, make sure that you are familiar with how to navigate any software that you're going to ask the teacher to use. Districts and schools often have student data saved into a common software that generates different reports. Before you meet with the teacher, make sure that you can pull their class data and run reports that give you the information you want to see.

Types of Data

Data Point	Action Item Scope	When to use
Assignments	Daily or weekly adjustments	This level of analysis is very closely related to data integration described above. If students are working on a major assignment, an essay, or a project, a data dive can help them make timely adjustments to their plans. Even if you want teachers to be more aware of how students are doing, you may use their independent practice activity to conduct a data dive. In either case, you would look at data from a student assessment or assignment given during a single lesson and help the teacher generate ideas for how to adjust instruction in future lessons.
Quizzes	Weekly adjustments	Quiz data helps the teacher determine adjustments to make within a unit. This is especially helpful for teachers who are not giving daily assessments. It lets them see that daily assessments help them correct misunderstandings before quizzes. It also helps teachers prevent major misunderstandings from derailing an entire unit. In this case, have teachers bring their weekly quizzes already graded to your meeting.
Unit Tests	2-6 Weeks	Teachers should be aware of their unit assessment data because it helps them predict how students might do on a benchmark exam or state test. It's also likely a large portion of a student's grade. Gaps from unit assessments are more difficult to fill because of the decreasing amount of instructional time that the teacher now has at their disposal. Luckily, units often build on one another, and teachers can re-address a concept when it comes up again in the next unit. To analyze unit assessments, it becomes especially important that a teacher have some sort of Excel file or tracking system and that the exams are already graded to save time to actually get to analysis.

Data Point	Action Item Scope	When to use
Benchmarks, Interim Assessments, or Common Assessments	Long-term	This is the most difficult type of data for new teachers to process because it is overwhelming. Benchmark exams and interim assessments are also the exams that are most important to administrators and district staff because they are most related to how students will perform on any high-stakes test given by the district or the state. These assessments often lead to more deeply rooted trends that create multiple action items. For instance, you might find that a teacher's highest achieving students are under-performing on big exams. That means they need to increase the rigor in their classroom, which involves a variety of steps implemented on a regular basis. When analyzing these larger exams, you and the teacher will likely need to pull reports from software used by the district or to use scanning devices to more easily score the exam.

One final consideration to include before you dive into data with a teacher is whether there are any campus or district initiatives that are a major focus at that time. This can be a good lens to use when analyzing data because it is a trend for the district and the teacher is likely already invested in addressing that trend. For example, the school may be focusing on its students with special needs and increasing their achievement. This focus automatically narrows the scope of your data dive and makes action items more achievable for the teacher. It also may relate to previous coaching items that they have had either from you or from other teacher educators. The steps below are recommended for what we see as the most appropriate forms of data to use for a data dive, but can be generalized to larger pieces of data.

Weekly Quizzes and Unit Assessments

In order to analyze data at this level, the teacher needs to have a tracking system. If the teacher doesn't have one, take the time to create it. Tracking student achievement regularly is an essential tool to analyzing data on a regular basis, which is necessary for improving instruction. See the steps to creating an Excel tracker on the next page.

Once you have the data in a manageable form, it's the coach's job to narrow the focus and look at specific aspects of student achievement. There are a couple of different options here:

Analysis by Question	Analysis by Standard	Analysis by Student Group
Look at the questions that had the highest percentage of correct answers and those that had the lowest percentage of correct answers. Identify the differences between those two sets of questions. It may be a difference in rigor or in the style of the question. It might also illuminate that students struggle with a particular question type or are not referring to supplementary information.	There may be two or more questions for each standard. Identify which standards students did the best on and what was happening in class when that standard was taught. Do the same for standards where students scored poorly. Analyze what was different about that class, and decide if those standards need to be re-taught in upcoming weeks or units.	Look at the individuals or groups of students who did well and those who did poorly, and see if any trends emerge. For example, you may find that students who are late to class struggled more, or that students who answered lots of questions in class did better. Those trends help you identify action items—creating a tardy policy, directing questions to a larger subset of students.

Following Up

Setting Goals

Goals should be data-centric. The action items you create from a meeting should be directly aligned to the gaps you saw in student achievement. You should also create a goal for the next time students take that type of assessment. For example, next time students take a weekly quiz, these four students should get a passing score OR the class average should improve by a certain number of points.

Create action steps aligned to that goal for both planning and execution. Make sure that the teacher incorporates any changes into their lesson plan and implements them skillfully in class. For example, if a teacher wants to have a review problem as their "Do First" in each class period, they need to plan that review problem and explain the correct answer to facilitate student exploration and discussion.

Natural teaching style reaches some students better than others, and teachers should be meeting the needs of all learners. For example, a teacher who has a degree in their content area may be naturally gifted at explaining material at a very rigorous level. They need to continue using their strength in rigor, and, at the same time, they need help breaking down material so that it's clear for every student in class.

Common Action Items

Because novice teachers develop their skills in a predictable way, action items coming from data dives are often aligned to their level of development. Keep in mind that data often leads you in a different direction than you had previously thought. Remember to stay open and see where data takes you. Here are a few of the action items that we find our coaches typically using:

Seating charts: Teacher and coach create a seating chart that places students in either heterogeneous or homogeneous groups. Heterogeneous groups are best for cooperative learning structures and for peer tutoring. Homogeneous groups should be created ONLY when the teacher is ready to differentiate content, process, product, and support for his or her students.

Scaffolding questions: Teacher and coach practice writing questions for a lesson that range from easier to more difficult questions. They may also create a system for directing these questions at different student groups to make sure a broader group of students is answering each question.

Differentiating content, process, product: Teacher and coach create resources for an upcoming lesson that are differentiated. They may differentiate a project for an upcoming unit or create differentiated independent practice worksheets to help push students on different levels.

Re-teaching and re-takes: Teacher and coach create a plan for tutoring or re-teaching. Concepts may need to be re-taught to a few students in tutoring or to an entire class. Teacher and coach may also create a system for students to re-test on that concept so that they can assess whether re-teaching helped improve student mastery.

Student data analysis: Teacher and coach create a way for students to track their own mastery and analyze their results. For example, students may enter their score for each objective into a tracker, and then choose practice activities that help them improve their skills on that objective.

Student output should drive the work of teachers. At Teaching Excellence, we strive to incorporate data in every coaching interaction and generally have data dive meetings with teachers at least once a year. Building the skill of analyzing student data facilitates independence for teachers and increases their ability to continue to improve their practice without a coach. Once a teacher is using data regularly, you'll see their practice become much more purposeful, and they'll see student achievement skyrocket.

1. Which teachers are ready for data integration coaching, and how will you approach student achievement data analysis with them? What systems for assessment do they have in place, i.e. exit tickets, weekly quizzes, etc.?

2. Which teachers need coaching to establish routines for assessing student learning? What routine will you prioritize with each of them (daily assessment or weekly assessment for example)?

3. Connect to the chapters 8 and 10, "Criteria for Success & Additional Considerations in a Debrief." Create some step-by-step criteria for successful data analysis to use with your teachers who are developmentally ready for this. Use the questioning strategies mentioned to prompt teacher reflection on action steps.

14

CHAPTER 14 **Following Up on the Debrief**

Teacher development is an iterative process in which continuous improvement is accomplished through a series of high-impact touch points. Follow-up provides the momentum that drives the process because it holds the novice teacher accountable for implementing the grows that were addressed in the previous interaction. Whether you leveraged a traditional observation and debrief, or a different coaching interaction, always follow up on the feedback you left a teacher to make sure it's being implemented to increase student success.

There is a parallel with testing. While some may view testing primarily as an assessment tool, cognitive research studies show that the act of frequent quizzing (and thus recalling) creates stronger connections than simply rereading the material to be memorized. In a similar way, when you follow-up with novice teachers (causing them to revisit the growth areas and take the relevant action steps), you help them to increase retention of the concepts or practices.

The type of follow-up you use can vary based on the type of touchpoint involved and the key lever discussed.

When to Follow-up

At the end of the debrief

You set the stage for follow-up in the closing section of a debrief meeting by clearly defining the action steps for the novice teacher and the accountability steps you as their coach will take. Check with the novice teacher to assure understanding and buy-in. A good litmus test to ensure you are wrapping up the debrief with clear action steps is that both you and the teacher should have something to write down as a next step. If the teacher is not somehow capturing their action steps, they either don't have a clear vision of what to do next, or they aren't bought into the idea that these steps are necessary. A simple strategy is to directly posit a question such as, "What are your action steps coming out of this meeting?" and listen to the teacher's response. As a show of good faith and reciprocity, this is also

155

an opportunity for you to voice your own action steps in terms of how you'll be following up.

After the debrief

The standard after-the-brief follow-up is to send the updated notes you have captured during the debrief to the teacher either by email or by uploading it to the campus feedback database. In addition, send an email that includes:

- A reference to a key point from the debrief or a personal connection to the teacher, such as, "Hope you do well in the marathon this weekend."
- The action steps that were agreed on.
- An invitation for questions or responses, such as, "Please send me an email if you have any questions or need help."

Copy relevant stakeholders as required (and agreed upon) to keep everyone involved in a teacher's development up-to-date and aligned.

In the next observation

Of course, you will be looking for implementation of the criteria for success in the next scheduled observation. However, you don't have to wait that long. If the practice went well during the debrief and the criteria for success is applicable to the beginning of the next class, you can stay in the room after the debrief to observe the results immediately. For example, if you worked on an entrance procedure, you can stay in the room to observe and give immediate written feedback aligned to what was practiced in the meeting. If that's not practical or applicable, you can always pop in on a class between scheduled observations just long enough to check on the implementation of a specific practice and provide immediate feedback via email or a handwritten note.

In the next debrief

In the logistics section of the debrief, review the action steps from the previous meeting and get an update from the teacher on their progress, asking questions to determine the impact on the classroom. Ideally the grow has become a glow. If so, encourage the teacher to share what actions they took that led to success. It's important for them to reflect on and realize how their actions led to results for students. This will provide encouragement for them to continue implementing the criteria for success and may help you identify effective coaching actions for yourself.

If the teacher hasn't implemented an action item and it is affecting the classroom, you should return to it and refine the practice and application so it really sticks this time. If you also noticed a different key lever, you can ask the teacher to implement both action items. When deciding a course of action, dig deeper to find the cause. Some of these deeper causes are discussed below.

Misidentified key lever. When developing the debrief, the key lever you identified may have been a symptom instead of the root cause. You may need to dig deeper to determine whether an underlying issue should be addressed first. This is sometimes the case when, for example, a teacher is having difficulty transitioning students from one activity or lesson component to another, resulting in a loss of instructional time. It is intuitive to identify a key lever based in the routines and procedures that the teacher has established (or lack thereof). However, it may be the case that the teacher generally lacks a sense of urgency and skills to impart that urgency to students. If this is the case, the existing routine they have may be adequate to the task, therefore re-tooling their routine could result in the same loss of instructional time. Coaching the teacher to use countdowns, timers, and positive behavior narration will help the teacher drive all future transition routines they implement with students.

Another misidentified key lever moment occurs when the original key lever may not have been developmentally appropriate for the teacher. This is often the case with instructional key levers. For example, if your goal is to help the teacher increase the rigor of their lessons, it might be more developmentally appropriate to coach them first on how to scaffold instruction before jumping straight into rigor.

Lack of motivation. This can happen in a situation where you haven't received buy-in before proceeding with practice and application. The teacher may have been disinvested from the start, but you failed to discern it. Look at Chapter 10: "Additional Considerations During the Debrief" for more ideas.

Lack of knowledge. This gap in information can be due to lack of clarity. You can avert this by asking questions during the practice and application section of the debrief to assure that the novice teacher fully understands the criteria for success and can model it authentically.

Lack of success. If the teacher implemented the action items without success and discards the practice, dig deeper to uncover the source of the problem. Perhaps they misunderstood how to implement it, or they aren't implementing the practice consistently and therefore aren't getting results. In this situation, a co-observation touchpoint with an experienced teacher can allow the novice teacher to visualize the positive impact the practice can have on a classroom when done well. Alternately, a video observation could be useful to enable them to see the evidence and rationale for proposing the practice. See more information on video observations in Chapter 11: "Alternate Touchpoints." You as the teacher educator may also need to reflect on the key lever you selected, the strategy and criteria for success you created, and the rationale you used to discover why your feedback didn't work for the teacher in this instance.

The follow-up can come in many shapes and sizes:

Email

If you have a positive relationship with the teacher, they may appreciate a follow-up email or note of encouragement related to the action step or mindset you discussed in the meeting.

Pop-in

One relatively easy way to follow up on an action item is to pop into a teacher's classroom for a few minutes in between longer scheduled observations just long enough to check on the implementation of a specific practice and provide immediate feedback via email or a handwritten note.

For example, your novice teacher struggled with projecting a strong presence in the class. He or she was soft-spoken, lacked confident body language, and generally failed to students accountable for off-task behavior, especially while giving instructions.

During the debrief, you focused on addressing the class with a strong voice and confident body language. After this debrief, you go into the classroom for short stretches of time over the next several days to observe progress. Leave quick feedback such as, "You spoke in a much louder voice than before, and that got students' attention. Now focus on proximity when giving instructions as a way of redirecting students who may be engaged in side conversations. By standing next to them, they are more likely to pause their off-task discussion and return their focus on you." The teacher educator observes for five to 10 minutes during these pop-ins, but because they occur once or twice a day for a week, the teacher receives frequent, nuanced feedback to better implement the strategy.

Pro-Tip: In the initial observation, you gathered data on student behavior and academic output to determine a key lever. In a pop-in, collect new data points so you can offer a comparison that quantifies the teacher's progress.

Assisted observation

Schedule an assisted observation with a stakeholder, such as the campus administrator or evaluator, to get the benefit of another pair of eyes. This touchpoint is especially useful for a situation where a campus evaluator had a concern about this teacher, and you have noticed improvement since the last evaluation.

Data dive

Schedule a data dive touchpoint to examine a set of student assessments to see the impact of the practice in comparison to previous practices or attempts. This is especially applicable if students have a major assessment coming up or if you've just worked on an instructional key lever. You can find more information on data dives in Chapter 13: "Data-Driven Coaching."

Lesson plan

Request that the teacher send you a lesson plan that demonstrates the criteria for success and provide feedback on how each criterion was implemented. This works best when the application portion of the debrief involved lesson planning.

Pro-Tip: Since this type of follow-up requires a significant effort, you should use it sparingly and strategically. You can also ask the teacher to highlight the areas where they used your feedback, for example, where they wrote in checks for understanding after introducing a key point. That helps you scan more quickly to the parts of the lesson plan that were discussed in the debrief.

Follow-up creates and maintains momentum toward mastery. By using the appropriate method and avenue for following up with your cohort, you are not only holding novice teachers accountable, but you are also pushing them to create stronger connections with the skills and strategies as they actively practice them and make them their own.

~ CHAPTER REFLECTION ~

1. Do you have a system that enables the teacher, the coach, and other official stakeholders to access notes from coaching conversations? How are you currently communicating focus areas to your teachers and these stakeholders?

2. Who is a teacher you've recently met with that might benefit from a quick pop-in observation as a follow up to that coaching conversation? Schedule this pop-in on your calendar.

3. Have you misidentified a key lever? Think of a teacher for whom it is challenging to coach. Was your recent key lever a symptom of a more pressing trend? Was your key lever too advanced?

15

CHAPTER 15 **Coaching Support Staff**

Many administrators and teacher educators coach or evaluate staff members who don't have a traditional teaching assignment but still work directly with students and contribute to student achievement. Some of these roles may include:

- Interventionists, such as staff who teach lower levels of reading, math, and writing or who pull small groups of students to help remediate previously taught concepts
- Special education teachers
- English language learning (ELL) coordinators
- Counseling and behavior staff
- Gifted and talented staff

These staff members have traditionally received less direct coaching from teacher educators, although their impact on student achievement is crucial. This chapter introduces ideas and strategies for coaching these staff members in a way that both values them as professionals and creates a more holistic learning atmosphere for students.

Lay the Groundwork

While there is significant overlap between coaching teachers and coaching support staff, there are also differences. Before you embark on an academic year that involves coaching support staff, take a moment to appreciate the adjustments you may need to make to the practices you've developed as a teacher educator.

Above all, coach

Support staff are usually added onto the load of a coach or evaluator in addition to teachers with traditional teaching assignments. They deserve just as much attention as any other teacher, so take care to build in equitable time to support your people. If you're unfamiliar with a staff member's job requirements, or assume they have more expertise than you, you may find yourself avoiding coaching interactions. In that case, develop the capacity and knowledge you need to better support your staff.

Develop a rubric

In addition to observing and collaborating with a mentor, consider using their expertise to create an evaluative tool such as a rubric or trajectory to measure the support staff member's development. The document you produce may help not only your support staff member to define what high quality support looks like for specific groups of students, it may also help others in your district or your region.

Join a professional organization

Join a professional organization along with the support staff member you are coaching. For example, a Council for Exceptional Children membership includes weekly email blasts and professional development opportunities that you and the staff member can take advantage of. Seek out trainings from state education agencies or from regional partners. For example, the state of Texas has Educational Service Centers in each region that provide ongoing professional development on a variety of topics. Having the teacher attend such trainings, or attending together, can help the teacher build necessary skills.

Hit the books

Do some research together and determine action items that help the support staff member improve their practice based on research. See Chapter 11 for more information on research touchpoints. Remember to rely on peer-reviewed research, which will both improve the staff member's practice and will give them a way to continue improving in the future.

Learn from a pro

Schedule co-observations of an accomplished staff member (in your network or the support staff member's network) or visit a school with an excellent gifted and talented, special education, intervention, behavior, or ELL program at least once per semester. Have your support staff member replicate the best practices that they see. See Chapter 11: "Alternate Touchpoints" for more information on co-observation touchpoints.

Find a mentor

Seek out someone who facilitated a training for your teacher, a district staff member, or another teacher at your school who is experienced and accomplished in the field. Leverage this person's leadership to help develop skills in others.

Focus on skills, but communicate beliefs

As mentioned in the introduction to this book, a set of core beliefs drives everything we do while coaching. It is crucial for the coach of a support staff member to have and communicate their beliefs about serving that population. As you coach, focus on skills, but communicate them through core beliefs—beliefs you bring to the job, beliefs you develop as you progress, and the beliefs of the organization. For example, you need to communicate to special education teachers your belief that students with special needs can reach achievement standards with support. Alternately, you should promote the belief that all students can behave, even if it may require support from counselors or behavior interventionists.

A teacher educator should have a strong opinion, based on research and best practice, about how students with special needs or English language learners should be served and educated. However, as you work with a teacher or staff member, focus on building skills that achieve outcomes. For instance, you may believe that restorative justice is the best type of behavior support. In that case, instead of spending a debrief discussing the idea with a behavior interventionist, build the skill of holding restorative justice circles. When support staff have the skills to deliver on an idea, they will automatically buy into the belief that it is best for students.

Evaluate on outcomes, not compliance

Many support staff members are required to complete paperwork and meet specific deadlines. For example, special education teachers have crucial responsibilities to submit detailed paperwork according to strict federal deadlines. While these responsibilities are incredibly important and are frequent topics of conversation, you should devote most of your time and attention to student outcomes and student growth. If all the paperwork is done, but vulnerable populations of students are failing or under-achieving, then the goal hasn't been achieved. It's a best practice to focus on compliance at the beginning of the year, and set teachers up with systems they can use on a regular basis. Then, you can move on to the specific skills they'll need to work with students. Don't shy away from accountability conversations about approaching deadlines, but make sure you are developing the staff member's skills for increasing student achievement.

Be aware of community or isolation

Many staff members who serve in support roles are the only person on their team. Even if they are part of a larger team, they may experience feelings of isolation because they are unsure of how they fit into the school community. Teachers with traditional assignments form bonds with their grade-level teachers or others who teach similar courses. Messages about best practices flow informally through these networks. Support staff may hear these messages only from their direct coach or manager. It's important to pass on information that other teachers pick up through these informal networks. For example, a special education teacher may have a class of seventh-grade students, but these students don't transition from room to room. They are isolated from their peers in a self-contained environment in the same way as the teacher, and so it is likely that the students and the teacher will miss announcements about upcoming field trips. You are responsible for assuring that this teacher is either participating in grade-level field trips or has the skill to plan their own.

Bridge the Gap

Teachers with traditional teaching assignments grow in a specific way and build skills over time. That's how Teaching Excellence derived the TE Rubric—by looking at predictable skills and growth gained over time. Support staff also grow in a predictable way. If you have served in a support role before, think about how you developed skills over the course of a school year, and create a rubric or trajectory document to help you chart a teacher's progress. If you have never worked in the same position as a support staff member, interview an accomplished professional who has, and create the a rubric or trajectory document together. In some cases, support staff can be coached and evaluated using the same rubric as general education teachers. See the end of this chapter for the sample Arc of Development for special education teachers.

Set goals

Goals should be set collaboratively and early in the year. You can use shared goals to coach the support staff member and evaluate their progress. For example, an ELL coordinator may set a goal that 100 percent of students will grow one or more levels on their state English Language Proficiency Assessment System exam that year and that 100 percent of staff members will use literacy strategies in their classroom. Over the year, a coach returns to these goals, assesses progress, and builds skills needed to attain them. For example, the coach may work with the ELL coordinator to present all-staff professional development on literacy strategies.

Meet before the year begins

It's always a good idea to meet with district staff members before the beginning of the year to discover their priorities. Build a vision of success for support staff and identify resources to help you coach your staff members. For example, your district may have a student support department. You should meet with the coordinator before the beginning of the year and continue to communicate regularly on how best to support a behavior interventionist or counselor. For more information on identifying resources, see Chapter 3: Building Stakeholder Relationships.)

Use all the resources at your disposal—research, training, and people—to build your belief about the best way to serve a specific student population. Beliefs are just as important for support staff as they are for other teachers.

Build relationships

Just as you do with any of your teachers, use every interaction with a support staff member as an opportunity to build a relationship. As mentioned above, keep in mind that these staff members often feel isolated from the larger school or district culture. Many of the professional development sessions and school-wide meetings offered to all staff do not account for the specific needs of support staff. So proactively include them and check in regularly to address their questions and needs. For example, at the beginning of each day of summer professional development, you could meet with the special education teachers to review the schedule of sessions that day and point out how each session applies to their role. Let them know where they can find you throughout the day to ask questions or get help. See Chapter 2: "Building Teacher Relationships," for more information.

Summer professional development

Summer professional development is a key time for establishing the framework for working with support staff.

Set priorities

For a support staff member to be successful, they should be prepared to navigate a typical day for this role. Set priorities for the first six weeks of school, particularly regarding skills they must acquire before the school year begins. These topics may include:

- Assessing students and determining their academic/behavioral/language level
- Reading and understanding how to complete and file the paperwork that will be required
- Creating and following a customized schedule
- Meeting with parents and other teachers at the school to create plans for students
- Building relationships with students

Set expectations

Show teachers the documents that you will be using to coach them, and be clear about what you will be looking for during the first six weeks of school or the first quarter of the school year. For example, you may want a counselor to conduct introductory staff training, gather student referrals, and create groups for counseling sessions by the end of the first month of the year.

Set the schedule

Many support staff use the first six weeks of the school year to determine which students they will serve and to create a schedule. They may not directly interact with students or stakeholders for a few weeks. This gap can make it difficult for you to understand how to best support them, what to observe, and what to meet about. You can use this time to schedule goal-setting conversations, help them test and evaluate students, work with them to create a schedule, or hold initial conversations with parents and students.

Once the first six weeks of the school year has passed, be clear about when you expect the support staff member to transition to serving students and how they should allocate their day between spending time with kids, meeting with stakeholders, or completing paperwork. This transition can be very difficult for some support staff members. It's a great time to schedule a co-observation with a mentor or at a school to get a better picture of the day.

Adapt

Coaching support staff requires you to be flexible and identify best practices for helping them progress in their career. These practices may go beyond concrete skills such as behavior management and instruction to engaging with others, leveraging influence, setting up systems, and other skills.

Worktime touchpoints

While TE recommends observing a teacher and then holding a debrief, support staff often have responsibilities that take longer than one 45-minute meeting to complete. You can schedule a worktime touchpoint, setting aside two 45-minute meetings to complete these bulkier responsibilities. For example, you can use a worktime touchpoint to complete individualized education program paperwork with a special education teacher or to create behavior plans for each student in the caseload of a behavior interventionist. Just make sure that there is an accountability component of the second touchpoint, such as having a staff member send you the final product for your review and feedback or attending the parent meeting where documents are discussed.

Practice

Practice often looks different for support staff than it does for traditional teachers. In application, TE typically requires traditional teachers to either write part of a lesson plan or to stand and deliver a portion of their lesson to solidify classroom skills. That type of practice doesn't always apply to support staff, though some aspects of this skill might be beneficial. Consider what a staff member would need to feel confident doing this skill on their own. You can replace application with a role play of a conversation with a student or stakeholder or develop resources that support staff can use in their day-to-day work.

Mindset

Because support staff often experience their impact on students through other adults, they must believe that their role includes building relationships with others and leveraging influence. Support staff frequently need to advocate for themselves or their students with other adults, such as other teachers or staff at the school, district staff, parents, and community organizations. Mastering this crucial skill will help them achieve better outcomes for students, and it begins with a mindset. For example, it is likely that an ELL coordinator will need to gather samples of student writing from teachers. Help the coordinator plan how to make this request of teachers and how they will create systems of accountability to ensure they are receiving the documentation they need.

In addition, support staff members often rely on teachers for information about how students are doing. A counselor may have an awkward parent meeting because a particular teacher doesn't provide them with regular grade reports and so they lacked the information required to have a successful meeting. You could help the counselor prepare for a direct conversation with that teacher to ensure they have the materials they need to do their work while not asking too much of their peer. See Chapter 11, the section on mindset conversations for more information.

Professional Development

You want to avoid the two extremes of professional development with your support staff—either excusing them from all school or district professional development or forcing them to participate in every session even if it doesn't apply to them. When support staff are excused from professional development or staff meetings, they may gain additional time to complete responsibilities, but they also increase their isolation and the potential for missing out on crucial information that could help them better support students. Also, skipping such meetings could cause resentment from other teachers. On the other hand, asking support staff to sit in professional development that doesn't apply to them makes them feel their time is wasted and that their needs don't matter. The ideal solution is to make sure that you have addressed your support staff's needs in professional development using the best practices below.

Pre-meetings

Meet with support staff beforehand and let them know that you want them to participate in professional development and how the professional development applies to their role. For example, you might say, "I want you to attend this session on creating student trackers. When the students get their grades this week, you should to be able to review their grades and help them make a plan to improve." Using this method, you can help staff members become more invested in attending the professional development and using the time to develop valuable resources.

Differentiated outcomes

When presenting the outcomes or goals of a session, you should include specific outcomes for support staff if they differ from the other participants in a session. For example, you might say to the whole group, "By the end of the session, you'll be able to create a student tracker for each of your kids. For our special education teachers and interventionists, you'll be able to support the use of the student trackers by having a one-on-one conversation with your students about their grades and helping students create action plans." Adding a goal for support staff, and additional rationale about how a skill applies to them, helps increase investment and ultimate use of that skill.

Targeted practice

In professional development sessions, there should always be a component when teachers are writing lesson plans or standing and delivering part of their lesson. For support staff, if it applies to their role, have them do the same practice. If not, give them a more appropriate task. For example, a reading interventionist who teaches six periods of small classes each day should do the same practice as the other teachers. A counselor, on the other hand, probably does not deliver lessons as often. In that case, provide them with another task so that they can still implement the skill. For example, the facilitator might say, "You now have 15 minutes to create your student trackers. To my three counselors in the room, I'd like you to create two things—an agenda for parent meetings about grades and a list of action items that students can use to write their commitments for improving their grades. When we stand and deliver, you will practice your parent conversations."

Support staff are integral to the success of a learning program, and as their coach, you must be willing to adapt your coaching practice and style for the unique challenges of their positions. When you do so, you not only facilitate their professional growth, but also increase the core strength of the educational atmosphere for all students. Coaching support staff well also highlights the power of growing and strengthening your entire coaching tool kit. As you become more adept at giving each teacher what they need, and in the method which speaks most clearly to them, you will see your entire cohort of novice teachers grow confidently into the profession. Now, we transition away from coaching to another incredibly valuable skill that most teacher educators are asked to use on a regular basis, but few are ever developed to use effectively: creating and facilitating adult learning opportunities.

1. Make a list of the support staff you work with. Have you directed them towards membership in a professional organization? If not, put this as an action step in your next meeting with them.

2. What goals do your support staff members have for the students they work with? What types of alternative touchpoints would be helpful in coaching them to achieve these goals?

3. What is the current state of professional learning opportunities for your support staff members? Are sessions differentiated with them in mind? Is there an upcoming opportunity from your campus or district to provide them with a more targeted session?

Appendix: Special Education Arc of Development

August	❏ Read Individualized Education Program (IEP) & Full Individual Evaluation (FIE) paperwork ❏ Request paperwork & hold Transfer IEPs ❏ Create student cover sheets ❏ Read unit plans and curriculum resources ❏ Tier objectives ❏ Initial meetings with general education teachers ❏ Plan and teach intervention classes
September	❏ Create schedules ❏ Hold regular meetings with general education teachers ❏ Conduct placement IEPs ❏ Plan for inclusion/pull-out services ❏ Roll out big goals to students ❏ Placement testing/diagnostic testing ❏ Progress monitor IEP goals
October	❏ Begin specially designed instruction ❏ Conduct annual IEP meetings ❏ Check-in with students regarding data ❏ Plan and conduct tutorials ❏ Data dive for Common Assessment 1
November/ December	❏ Conduct annual IEP meetings ❏ Revise schedules based on data ❏ Check-in with students regarding data ❏ Hold regular meetings with general education teachers ❏ Plan and conduct tutorials ❏ Plan and teach classes

January	❏ Conduct annual IEP meetings ❏ Follow inclusion schedules with fidelity ❏ Check-in with students regarding data ❏ Hold regular meetings with general education teachers ❏ Plan and conduct tutorials ❏ Progress monitor IEP goals ❏ Plan and teach classes
February	❏ Conduct annual IEP meetings ❏ Follow inclusion schedules with fidelity ❏ Check-in with students regarding data ❏ Hold regular meetings with general education teachers ❏ Plan and conduct tutorials ❏ Data dive for Common Assessment 2 ❏ Plan and teach classes
March	❏ Revise IEP goals ❏ Conduct annual IEP meetings ❏ Revise inclusion schedules ❏ Check-in with students regarding data ❏ Hold regular meetings with general education teachers ❏ Conduct tutorials ❏ Plan and teach classes
April	❏ Finalize work portfolios ❏ Conduct annual IEP meetings ❏ Follow inclusion schedules with fidelity ❏ Check-in with students regarding data ❏ Hold regular meetings with general education teachers ❏ Conduct tutorials ❏ Plan and teach classes
May	❏ Close IEP paperwork ❏ Follow inclusion schedules with fidelity ❏ Finalize goal reflections with students ❏ Complete final project/portfolio with students ❏ Meet with teachers for final feedback ❏ Plan and teach classes

16

The Professional Learning Core Beliefs

Up to this point, this book has focused on the micro environment: the interactions that take place between a teacher and their coach and the feedback necessary to ensure they are growing for their students. With YES Prep and the Teaching Excellence (TE) program, as it is in many school systems across the country, this is not the entire puzzle. Teachers need ongoing professional development, too. We also pull teachers together for two weeks during the summer and once a month throughout the year to participate in whole-group and small-group professional development. While all teacher educators within TE participate in the facilitation of these sessions, a subset of team members called the Professional Learning team create the sessions. It is our opinion that their work lays the foundation upon which our teacher educators and teachers build their one-on-one coaching relationships. This section of the book begins with an overview of our beliefs about professional learning and progresses into the harder skills of writing sessions and developing yourself and others as exemplary facilitators for adult audiences. Even if you do not have a team of session writers, you can use the beliefs, skills, and strategies that follow to facilitate engaging professional learning that catalyzes teacher growth.

Professional Learning Must Create Change

Whether you support a grade level, a content team, a campus, or a district, the time that your entire team spends together should be viewed as sacred. The opportunities to pull all the teachers you support together are never frequent or long enough. It is therefore crucial to get the most impact from the limited time you do have. Because our Professional Learning team operates with this belief, we subsequently create sessions and adult learning opportunities that are designed to target a specific gap in teacher practice and lead to predetermined change. By constantly working from this mindset, we regularly find that student outcomes are improved because of purposeful time spent together with teachers who are engaged in a meaningful learning experience.

As any child can tell you, it's not what you say, but what you do that shows what you really believe. The tone and atmosphere surrounding the spaces during the time your entire team is engaged in the same task will ultimately be the tone that is associated with that team by its members.

We believe that consistent modeling of researched-based best practices is the most powerful method of mentoring teacher educators. It is frustrating for teachers (or any adult learner) to be unsure of how to tackle a specific problem, or what a specific strategy looks like when put into practice. We work to ensure every educator knows what success looks like and how to achieve it; therefore, every session includes some type of facilitator model. Models may take the form of think-alouds, facilitator acting, or exemplar teacher videos. We discuss the specifics of session writing in Chapter 18.

Furthermore, we model the level of professionalism we expect to ultimately see in the classroom, down to the quality of the materials we develop for Professional Learning sessions and communications with stakeholders. All members of our Professional Learning team work from a common set of templates when creating presentations, handouts, and other deliverables so that all touchpoints with the team reinforce the message of excellence.

Elements of Exemplary Professional Learning Sessions

The following ideals are the lenses through which the Professional Learning team at TE views all sessions. In attempting to maximize all of these elements, our sessions become more likely to result in teacher-level change, and student-level success.

Clear and engaging. Training for novice teachers is no place for theoretical conjecture. It must be concrete with clear application in the classroom. Keep the language simple. For example, saying to a room full of teachers, "Teacher models exist to give students an exemplary method for completing a stated objective" is not nearly as effective as stating "Model the skill to students." Research into adult learning also states that all learners retain content better when they are actively involved in an engaging, entertaining session with a clear topic and outcome. Teachers have a variety of demands on their time, and we want them to feel that time spent in professional development is both enjoyable and beneficial. A typical Teaching Excellence session may allow for opportunities for teachers to discuss challenges with peers, evaluate and provide feedback on the practice of others, practice implementing a new skill into their planning or instruction, or explain a new concept in their own words to aid in retention. No more than one third of a standard session is spent in a stereotypical sit-and-get format. An effective session should feel more like an effective classroom lesson and less like a college lecture.

Building to practice. A teacher attempting to implement a new skill needs a venue for practicing the skill before executing it in the classroom. In a training session, facilitators provide feedback to increase the likelihood of successful implementation. We operate under the assumption that a ball that begins rolling in a session is more likely to continue rolling in a classroom, and a ball that doesn't start moving with support stands little chance of moving without that support the next day. Time to practice the targeted skill and opportunities for teachers to receive feedback on their practice should be built into every session.

Developmentally appropriate. It is not enough to present a well-thought-out session if the audience is not ready for its content. The Professional Learning team takes great effort to ensure that the scope and sequence of their sessions dovetails with the tiers of the rubric that we use to develop our teachers. As a rule of thumb, we try to keep whole-group professional learning a step or two ahead of one-on-one coaching. For example, from the beginning to end of October, many of our novice teachers are planning at a solid level and are prepared to begin thinking about adjusting course mid-lesson based on student mastery. Therefore, our September Professional Learning Saturday typically focuses on crafting aligned and engaging checks for understanding. When our Professional Learning team does this successfully, teachers avoid feeling helpless because they have some techniques in their arsenal of teacher practices to try when faced with a developmentally appropriate issue. In October, when teachers have the skill to notice students who are confused during practice, they are already able to craft checks for understanding to identify misunderstandings earlier in the lesson. Further, our coaches can save time for application in debriefs because less time needs to be spent on discussing the issue itself. In the world we hope to create, that common vocabulary was built during the previous month's professional development sessions.

Focused on facilitation. Keep in mind that you are a teacher educator, not a public speaker. At all levels, the content is king. The presenter is merely a conduit. Surely a great facilitator is engaging, however, a great facilitator ensures that the stickiest parts of any session are related to the content of the session rather than the stage presence of the facilitator themselves. The Professional Learning team spends a great deal of time thinking about and learning about the best ways of teaching adults in a large-group setting, and we hope that the following chapters will help you tackle that learning curve more quickly than we did!

Continuously Improve

Just as the research on adult learning evolves, so do our teachers, so do our teacher educators, and so must we. Our Professional Learning team uses several methods to ensure that our saw stays sharp as we write new Professional Learning sessions and help other facilitators develop themselves.

Leverage data

The Professional Learning team works to ensure that all their decisions are rooted in data, from how we develop facilitators to how we structure sessions. We constantly work with our colleagues on campuses and at the district level in an attempt to obtain new and better data from which to inform our decision making. In the past, this has taken the form of looking at teacher-level evaluation data and student-level test scores or item analyses, and then noting the type of questions students get incorrect the most often. While intuition is frequently helpful, especially for experienced educators, objective data has the final word. Humility can be the best ally of the educator. Growth often follows diligent research that fails to confirm your beliefs.

Incorporate feedback

Because we believe in the sanctity of all instances where groups of educators are investing their time, we encourage all teacher educators who present sessions to teams to seek feedback at every stage, from development to execution. Feedback conversations and surveys are powerful tools to determine the best structure for a session targeted to novice teachers, helping guide decisions such as determining how much time to spend on application or the best way to engage teachers while ensuring that the focus of a session is the material.

Refine through assessment

Any important endeavor, including professional learning, must be held accountable to its results. This can be especially challenging in regard to professional learning because it is often a smaller part of a teacher educator's responsibilities and rarely a strength that a new teacher educator is equipped with when assuming their new role." We believe that improvement comes through honest assessment. With that in mind, our facilitators are held accountable to the satisfaction of their teachers if for no other reason than that dissatisfied teachers are less likely to implement the skills and strategies presented. And for the same reason, the Professional Learning program itself must be held accountable to the satisfaction of the facilitators and the teacher-level implementation of their sessions' content. We use teacher-rubric data to measure the actual effectiveness of our sessions at the team, facilitator, teacher and, when possible, the student level.

Keep learning

The Professional Learning program provides professional development not only to teachers but also to facilitators. Consequently, the Professional Learning team regularly attends professional development and keeps up to date on current research, both in adult learning and teacher development, to stay on the leading edge of research and current practices.

Now that the lenses we use to approach our work have been discussed, we encourage you to view the remaining Professional Learning chapters through them and determine which of the following tools and skills would help you in your context as you develop your teachers through adult, group learning.

1. Recall an especially productive and memorable professional learning experience in which you've participated in the past. Which of these core beliefs were present? How did they impact you as a participant?

2. Similarly, recall a professional development opportunity you've participated in that was memorable because of its *lack* of productivity or engagement. How could the infusion of one or more of these beliefs have helped you more authentically engage with the content?

3. New members of our team sometimes hesitate to fully embrace the idea of seeking out as much feedback — both positive and critical — as possible. What, in your opinion, is the danger in failing to do so — both for the teacher educator and the teacher alike?

17

CHAPTER 17 **Creating a Scope and Sequence**

In a classroom, a scope and sequence is a foundational document for a teacher that defines:

- the elements (knowledge, skill, mindset) required for a student to master a subject
- the time allotted for instruction (units, six weeks, a quarter, an academic year)
- the order in which the elements are presented

A scope and sequence codifies for that teacher, and makes clear for everyone else, where the priorities lie for that content in that classroom. With it, the teacher can more purposefully spend their time in the classroom, more accurately determine how close their students are to predetermined goals, and make the most informed course adjustments when necessary. It is difficult for most teacher educators to imagine a successful classroom that does not have an aligned, regularly referenced scope and sequence.

At TE, we operated for too long without a scope and sequence for the development of novice teachers. We simply measured our teachers' progress along the rubric rows on which they were evaluated and then argued at the end of the year about how successful we had been. We were reactionary.

Since the development of our new teacher trajectory and aligned scope and sequence, we can continually assess our progress to predetermined goals. We can be proactive. We have also become a more effective program all around, as the scope and sequence that informs the Professional Learning sessions also informs all learning experiences for developing teachers, from their onboarding/orientation sessions, to independent assignments, to the one-on-one coaching touchpoints that teachers have with their teacher educator.

While in the following pages we explain how we created our scope and sequence at a programmatic level, know that any teacher educator can use a similar set of steps to create a similar tool for any team of teachers. In other words, while a district administrator can use these steps to determine the best way to onboard, support and train the new teachers at many schools effectively, one grade-level chair on one campus can use the same set-up steps to ensure that their team effectively builds culture, plans events, and strengthens family and community relationships throughout the year.

Who Creates a Scope and Sequence and When

Any good scope and sequence should be created proactively. At TE, our Professional Learning team uses our scope and sequence from the previous year, along with data such as teacher results and feedback, when creating the next iteration. Once you make the initial investment in time, revisiting this tool prior to the start of every new school year becomes an incredibly powerful experience. If you do not have such a document in your toolkit now, it is our hope that you will feel the same sense of drive and relief that we felt the first time we put all our goals on the same piece of paper in an order that made sense. Whether you are creating this tool from scratch or revisiting an existing document, we recommend seeking input from as many stakeholders as possible along the way. Depending on your context, this could be people at the state, district, community, content, campus, or grade level. Be sure to seek the advice of peers who have similar responsibilities.

How to Create a Scope and Sequence

Scope: Start with your goals

The scope element of a scope and sequence is grounded in the goals you are responsible for achieving with your teachers. As we have discussed previously in this book, at TE, our teacher development goals are based in a rubric that defines the practices of an effective teacher. Since the TE program focuses on novice teachers, the goals we set for our teachers are at the "effective" level of this rubric, even though the rubric has a column above this. To take a practical approach, think about specific teachers or groups of teachers with whom you've worked in the past. When we plan our scope and sequence, we think about our teachers in quartiles. Then we ask ourselves what instruction, support and intervention would be needed for our average teacher (50th percentile or third quartile) to achieve the same outcomes as our above-average (75th percentile or 2nd quartile) teachers are currently achieving. For example, if one of the major differences we notice between our average and above-average teachers is the quantity and quality of the feedback they provide to their students, we might adjust our future scope and sequence to present this idea earlier in the year, or potentially more often. If we do this successfully over time, the performance of our cohort will consistently improve, as will the results of our students

The more concrete you make your goals, the easier it will be to create a scope and sequence. Our rubric, has been refined many times over the years, and we have worked with it long enough to have a very clear understanding of what our goals look and sound like when lived out in classrooms. The rubric identifies for us the knowledge, skills, and mindsets required for a teacher to meet the goals we have for them and their development. Breaking goals down in this way helps us plan for how we will help teachers reach these ends.

Knowledge. What does a teacher need to **know**? For example, a novice teacher must understand the *purpose* and *components* of a strong objective. These are lessons that teachers can demonstrate their mastery of through a survey or in discussion.

Skills. What does a teacher need to be able to **do**? For example, a teacher must be able to *write* and *communicate* a daily lesson objective. A teacher must actually practice a skill in order to demonstrate the accomplishment of this goal.

Mindsets. What does a teacher need to **believe**? For example, a teacher must *believe* that the goal of each lesson is to drive student achievement or mastery of an objective. This is the hardest element to assess, and can only be done through observing a combination of a teacher's words and actions. Even though this is difficult, knowing that a certain mindset is necessary for a goal to be met does allow us to effectively plan for such a goal in our scope and sequence.

Next, group these elements into categories and find themes that convey the categories. For example, the knowledge of the components of a strong objective, the skill of writing and communicating that strong objective for students, and the belief that every lesson should drive toward the mastery of a strong objective can be grouped into the theme of daily lesson planning. Similarly, the knowledge of the components of an effective behavior management system, the skill of positively reinforcing student behavior, and the belief that a strong classroom culture is necessary for students to learn can be grouped into the theme of classroom management and culture. These themes are not complete, and your examples may look different if your goals with novice teachers are different. However, having these themes (daily lesson planning, classroom management and culture, etc.) fleshed out will allow you to progress from the content of your plan to the sequence.

Sequence: Create a timeline

We next place the elements we have developed in the order that will most effectively build competence in the classroom. For example, teachers need to write a lesson plan before they can deliver a lesson, so we place the basic elements of lesson planning before the basic elements of lesson delivery. We then map the sequence into a time frame dictated by our context. TE is a one-year program, so all necessary categories/themes are mapped to a ten-month period. If you are a campus or district leader working with novice teachers, you have quite a bit more flexibility, as you can space things out into a two- or three-year trajectory. As you place these themes in your time frame, consider context. Sometimes, context can feel like a constraint. For example, during district assessments, due dates for report cards may affect the amount of time available to work with or observe teachers. However, the same context can be used to your benefit in helping your teachers. In the situation above, spending the little development time we have with teachers on data analysis or small group remediation not only gives teachers valuable skills, but will likely be well received by your audience as it is what they're thinking about anyway.

Once you create the timeline, consider the degree of repetition required for each element. Some categories, such as classroom management, may require multiple learning experiences in varying contexts, including teacher onboarding, Professional Learning sessions, independent assignments, and one-on-one coaching. You may also repeat topics, introducing more advanced material each time you touch upon them. We revisit lesson delivery several times throughout a given school year, starting from how to stand and clearly state the key points of a lesson through how to most effectively respond to correct and incorrect student responses.

The last question to ask yourself before finalizing your scope and sequence is which skills must be learned before the school year starts and which can be learned throughout the year. At TE, we have two weeks of professional learning time with our teachers before they set foot in the classroom. If you only have a few days, it's even more important to create clear goals and outcomes for this time. We ask ourselves: What do teachers need to believe, know, and do to be successful on Day One in the classroom? The phrase "Day-One Ready" is our frequently-articulated drive with teachers and with each other during those two weeks.

When done properly, a scope and sequence provides guidance and structure throughout an entire academic year. At the same time, it isn't a static document. It requires regular, hopefully small, adjustments based on feedback throughout the academic year. Use data such as teacher surveys, evaluations, student data, or parent and stakeholder feedback to adjust categories and themes or the order of the knowledge, skills and mindsets. For example, you might review elements that teachers did not master, or you might adjust the order of topics based on teacher or student performance data.

Sample Scope and Sequence

The Teaching Excellence Professional Learning scope and sequence covers a two-week summer "Induction" and one six-hour Saturday per month, as shown on following pages.

The first chart is a portion of a one-pager we put together to indicate the knowledge, skills, and mindsets that administrators can expect their teachers who have gone through our induction to possess when they arrive on campus. Our induction is broken into themes of sessions including culture, instruction, professionalism, and certification. These themes provide the lens through which the Professional Learning team approaches the summer onboarding. The "Instruction" scope and sequence is shown below. Notice the difference between the topics covered before the school year starts and those that are not covered until teachers have had an opportunity to practice these foundational skills and get to know their students.

The second chart is our scope and sequence for our Saturday sessions. The "Topic" column shows the theme for the month, which aligns to our scope and sequence. The "Priority" column shows the session that we require all teachers to attend to receive foundational knowledge, skills, and mindsets about the theme. Afterwards, our teachers select one session from the "Choice" column to further their learning and deepen a skill. Teachers are occasionally provided input about which session to select by their teacher educator or administration. Some sessions are repeated to accommodate teachers who may be ahead of, or falling behind, the scope and sequence or for teachers who were hired later in the school year.

Instruction Induction (Pre-Service) Session Scope	
Instruction Domain	Outcomes • Teachers will write lessons 5-Step or PDP lessons that align to objectives. • Teachers will summarize the key content ideas that need to be taught in the first six weeks of school.
	Content Internalization and External Alignment Sessions: • Take Summative Assessment • Internalizing Long-Term Plan • Take Unit 1 Assessment • Key Knowledge and Skills from Unit 1 • Internalizing Unit 1 Plans • Lesson Planning 1.0 • Content-Specific Skill Sessions
	Core Lesson Planning Sessions: • Introduction to Bloom's Taxonomy • Objectives • Exit Tickets • Key Points • Practice
	5-Step Lesson Cycle Sessions: • 5-Step Lesson Overview • Opening • Introduction to New Material with Checks for Understanding Planning • Checks for Understanding Execution • Guided and Independent Practice • Closing
	PDP Lesson Cycle Sessions: • PDP Lesson Overview • Pre-Reading • During Reading: Close Reading and Chunking • Checks for Understanding - Planning • Checks for Understanding - Execution • Post-Reading

Ongoing Professional Learning Scope and Sequence

Month	Topic	Priority Session	Choice Sessions
Aug	Culture 2.0	Sense of Urgency	• Behavior Management Cycle Overview • Culture Reflection and Problem-Solving Protocol • Increasing Student Motivation • Increasing Student Joy in the Classroom • Handling Severe Management Issues • Building Teacher and Student Leaders • Planning and Executing Academic Routines
Sep	Direct Instruction	Teacher Modeling and Think-Alouds	• Lesson Planning Overview • Direct Instruction Execution Protocol • 6 Strategies for Increasing Student Retention • Anticipating Student Misunderstandings • Increasing the Utility of Your Physical Environment • Brain-Based Learning • Accommodations and Modifications for the General Educator
Oct	Student Processing and Practice	Planning and Delivering Criteria for Success	• Student Practice Overview • Structuring Effective Practice • Effective Use of Time • Think, Pair, Share, and Turn & Talks • Increasing Student Success with Rubrics • Using Student-Level Trackers • Foldables for Engagement and Retention
Nov	Data Analysis	Planning and Implementing Data-Driven Checks for Understanding	• Using Mail Merge for Student Feedback • Creating Mastery Trackers • Using Student-Level Trackers • Questioning Strategies that Drive Mastery • Structuring Effective Practice
Jan	Ratio	Increasing Participation Ratio	• Promoting Critical Thought • Review Games & Strategies • Questioning Strategies that Drive Mastery • Foldables for Engagement and Retention • Executing an Effective Classroom Reset • Using Student-Level Trackers

Ongoing Professional Learning Scope and Sequence			
Month	**Topic**	**Priority Session**	**Choice Sessions**
Feb	Reaching All Learners	Introduction to Differentiation	• Accommodations and Modifications for the General Educator • Workstations in the Secondary Classroom • Small Groups in the Secondary Classroom • Advanced Routines and Procedures for Group Work • Differentiating Student Practice • Skillfully Scaffolding with Blooms Taxonomy
Mar	Rigor	Increasing Academic Rigor	• Promoting Critical Thought • Increasing Student Success with Rubrics • Project-Based Learning • Promoting Academic Discussion • Planning for Year 2 • Direct Instruction Execution Protocol • Review Games and Strategies • Questioning Strategies that Drive Mastery

Clearly, creating two documents each year with this level of purpose and detail is time-intensive. However, the alternative is to build the plane as we fly it. Given the tremendous number of important tasks on the plate of any teacher educator, we find the latter plan untenable, as it would not ensure that our teachers are developing as quickly and as effectively as possible. Of course, each month we assess our progress and make small adjustments to ensure that our ultimate goals are still within reach. The lion's share of our time, however, is spent writing, editing, internalizing, and facilitating high-quality professional learning opportunities for our teachers. We'll cover each one of these steps in detail as we present our process to you so that you can make your own practice even more effective for your teachers.

~ CHAPTER REFLECTION ~

1. What content or skills are you charged with delivering or imparting to your cohort of teachers? Be as exhaustive as you think will be helpful.

2. What benchmarks naturally occur within the timeframe you're considering? These might be the start of school, long breaks in the school year, major assessments, or teacher evaluation windows. List these benchmarks chronologically.

3. Which content or skill must be imparted to your teachers prior to each benchmark? When does each piece of knowledge or each skill make the most sense in the development of your teachers?

4. Were there noticeable gaps in your cohort of teachers last year that should be addressed earlier in the year when you sit down to do this same process for the upcoming school year?

18

CHAPTER 18 **Session Writing**

"Writing is nothing less than thought transference, the ability to send one's ideas out into the world, beyond time and distance, taken at the value of the words, unbound from the speaker." —Arthur M. Jolly

A session is a self-contained unit of professional learning. It presents the basic mindset, knowledge, and skills a teacher requires to effectively lead students to mastery of objectives, and then provides an opportunity to practice those skills. If you believe, like we do, that any time that you bring teachers together is sacred, then a session is the road map to ensure that all of this time is spent purposefully and in pursuit of the goals of the audience. You might think of a session as the professional learning equivalent of a lesson plan, and just like with an exemplary lesson plan, a session must have concise outcomes, clear instruction, and aligned practice.

A clear and engaging session can be an initial point of contact between teachers and a new teaching strategy, allowing them to acquire new strategies to apply in the classroom. For example, after a session about building a sense of urgency, a teacher should have a few more tools to increase their effectiveness. After completing an entire scope and sequence of sessions, teachers should be well-equipped to succeed in the classroom.

Additionally, a session can serve as a reference point for coach and teacher alike when a teacher struggles with a strategy. For example, if a teacher has challenges in executing teacher models, the coach can refer back to and review the practices in the relevant Professional Learning session to prepare for the debrief instead of creating that content from scratch.

Elements of a Session

An effective session:

Is clear and direct. A session isolates the discrete pieces of knowledge, skills, or mindsets and transmits those to teachers. At TE, we frequently use the concepts of chunking and grouping to break down the main concepts or skills and arrange them for maximum effectiveness. For example, in a session about creating and using checks for understanding during a lesson, we would explain the process of creating the checks during planning and using them while questioning during instruction. The session would explain these two processes independently so that we could clearly state each step. We work to avoid discussing topics that are so broad that they cannot be adequately covered in the time allotted. Instead, we isolate component parts of the topic and prioritize which are most important for teachers to know or be able to do in their next lesson.

Is concise and digestible. At TE, the person who facilitates a session is frequently *not* the person who wrote it. A facilitator should be able to internalize a session within a few hours. This places the burden on the writer to provide detailed notes for the facilitator, creating a script that allows the facilitator to focus on memorizing or internalizing the content instead of creating it. When we use PowerPoint, we include detailed instructions and scripts within the "notes" section of a slide. Facilitators can change the actual words of a session while they internalize, so long as the overall message remains. This allows the topic to be immediately clear to the audience and increases their focus and success when implementing any strategy.

Because we don't want our facilitators spending copious amounts of time on the PowerPoint itself, we pay special attention to how we explain the purpose of visuals and practice. For example, if a slide contains a picture of a pencil and paper, we include a clear note about the application of the image to the content so the facilitator doesn't have to guess. The pencil and paper could refer to the teacher making a checklist, to students taking a test, or to the need to write in pencil so you can erase. We take pains to clarify our intent when choosing an illustration.

The goal here is to codify sustained best practices that can be easily transmitted to teachers. If you write and facilitate professional learning yourself, we would still recommend these same practices so that you can facilitate the session again in future years, pass it along to another facilitator, or share it with participants so they can return to the key ideas.

Contains time for practice. Nothing cements a concept or a skill in the mind like practice. Schedule ample time in the session for teachers to practice and apply the specific knowledge, skills or mindset covered in the session. For example, once a teacher has seen the process for creating checks for understanding, allow the teachers to practice writing them into lesson plans and introducing them in execution. Too often, we see teacher educators cram as much information as possible into the time allotted, without saving time for application. We find that this leads to spotty follow-through on the part of the audience members. We strive to save at least a third (20 minutes of every hour) of all sessions to provide time for teachers to practice applying what they have learned.

Share the Load

The process of creating a new session is known as "session writing." At TE, session writing is the province of the Professional Learning team, who shares in the development of new sessions. If you have a team of people who specialize in this skill, or if you share session writing responsibilities across a few different administrators, content experts, or grade-level chairs, we offer a few tips on parceling out the load.

Not all sessions are created equal in terms of level-of-effort. Take into consideration the relative writing load required for all the sessions in a scope and sequence and assign them accordingly.

Leverage the knowledge, skill, and experience of each member of the Professional Learning team. For example:
- Assign a session about workstations to a member with experience teaching at the elementary level.
- Assign a session about accommodations and modifications to a member with experience teaching students with special needs.
- Bring in non-Professional Learning staff members with the capacity and pedagogical expertise to write a session.

Creating a Session

At TE, the process for developing a session proceeds in a four-week cycle. There are several reasons for this. Chief among them is the fact that, as mentioned before, the facilitators of our sessions are not necessarily the same people who write them. If you write sessions that only you will ever facilitate, then this process can be accelerated, as the level of detail in your notes need not be as fleshed out, and you will not have to start from scratch when internalizing it. The process of actually writing the session jumpstarts the internalization process. Another reason we use a four-week cycle is that we gather our teachers together one Saturday a month for professional learning, so it aligns with our context. Each week has a specific focus:
- Week one: Marshall resources.
- Week two: Create a first draft.
- Week three: Create a final draft.
- Week four: Facilitators internalize their session.

Marshall resources

During the first week, focus your efforts on laying the foundation:
- Reference the scope and sequence to see where teachers should be this time of year
- Identify and clearly explain the gap to be addressed
- Research the topic for potential content
- Gather resources to assist in development and presentation (these can be physical or human—don't discount the other experts at your disposal)
- Create an outline of the session

The first step is to identify the pedagogic need that the session is meant to fill, taking into account the developmental level of your teachers and the specific context you have about their performance. The session should be aligned to the scope and sequence, which is itself based on a rubric designed to vet topics for relevance. Once you have established need and relevance, evaluate the topic to verify that it can be covered in the allotted time. For example, if you're developing a 60-minute session, you don't have time to clearly present the large and unwieldy topic of academic rigor in an engaging manner, but you do have time to clearly present one facet of that topic—the idea of complex tasks.

Next, state the desired outcome in a simple sentence, such as:
- Teacher will be able to use checks for understanding to assess the effectiveness of a lesson.
- Teacher will be able to explain the process for planning a teacher model.
- Teacher will be able to plan a complex task for an upcoming class project.

Now it's time to do some research and gather resources. Interview people, look for student work samples, observe classes, read literature to gain a complete perspective on the topic. Take extensive notes. When possible, attend professional development to expand your understanding and learn best practices for educating teachers.

Outline the session

Once you have absorbed the essential material for the topic, the single most effective step you can take is to outline the session. An outline is the workhorse of session writing. Time spent here will pay off, because once you begin writing, the outline will guide each step and the application will practically roll off your fingers.

As you outline, visualize the structure of the session, the basic elements of presentation, and how they flow to create the most effective method of engaging and galvanizing your audience.

Pro-Tip: Because writing is an intensive process, it's important to commit to a session structure at the outset, because once the writing process starts, changing the structure is time-consuming. For example, if you decide to use a video to show a routine for collecting papers, you must be prepared to engage in the time-consuming and labor-intensive task of producing or finding a video. If you decide midstream that the routine for picking up papers would be better communicated by having the facilitator model the process during the session, then you will have to write-off all the effort spent on the video. So, it's important to commit to the structure of the session during outlining, so as to not waste time.

One common structure consists of:
- Introduction
- Hook/big idea
- Rationale/relevance
- Benefits/outcomes
- Presentation
- Practice
- Closing summary

While this is the order that the session will proceed from the participants' point of view, this is not the order in which we recommend actually writing the session.

Once your outcomes are firmly established, we recommend that you start with practice. Ideally, that practice will show you that teachers are making strides toward closing the gap you identified. Planning in this way ensures that when you create your instruction, you communicate only what is necessary to be successful on that practice and do not spend extra time communicating information that is only tangentially related to the session's topic. You can use the checklist at the end of this section to help you create sessions.

Practice. Determine the appropriate practice for the session to achieve the desired outcome. For example, if the outcome is that teachers will use checks for understanding to assess the effectiveness of a lesson, practice should involve teachers using checks for understanding to actually determine how well the students understand the key points.. Practice is the heavy-lifting portion of the session. During practice, teachers can stand and deliver the part of the lesson they have been working on with peer feedback. They may also write or edit their lesson plans based on a new skill, and then share with peers.

Knowledge and skills. Determine the knowledge and skills specific to the gap that will empower teachers to affect positive student outcomes. For example, when presenting the key points of how to write and deliver effective checks for understanding, the process could include:
- Review the key points and turn them into questions
- Structure the questions to involve all students (multiple choice or open-ended)
- Draft the ideal student response
- Use Bloom's Taxonomy to check the difficulty level of questions across the lesson

Presentation Structure. Tailor the presentation to the nature of the topic. For example, the session might use a model or a video to communicate the information. In the case of checks for understanding, the facilitator can explain some of the steps followed by practice, and then present the remaining steps followed by more practice. This portion of the session is facilitator-heavy. It should give participants everything they need to be successful on the designed practice and no more!

Rationale. Develop a rationale related to the audience that facilitates buy-in. The rationale helps teachers visualize the benefit of incorporating a strategy in their classroom. Too often, session writers include too much rationale. Think about your audience and what will ensure that they are bought into the session. Are they prone to respect research, or will emotional stories drive home the need of the topic more clearly? Interviewing students can help teachers see how the current gap is manifesting itself at a student level, motivating participants engage fully in the session. Pick the rationale that works best for your audience, and place it toward the beginning of your session chronologically. If you save it for the end, you risk late buy-in from teachers and consequently less engagement during instruction.

SPICE. You can add spice (strategies designed to capture attention) to a session by including one or more of the following:

- Story
- Personal experience
- Inspiration
- Challenge
- Enthusiasm

We save this step for this stage in the process so that we have a better understanding of the pacing of the session. If the session is tight, we may only endeavor to squeeze in one of these elements. However, we have found through trial and error that inserting one of these per roughly 20 minutes of session works best for creating an engaging session squarely focused on the content rather than the facilitator's presence.

Pro-Tip: When incorporating SPICE, give an example to help other facilitators develop an element that aligns with the session. For example, if you want a facilitator to tell a story about how failing to use timers during a lesson led to disaster, include an example story in the notes as a guide. Writing "tell a story" doesn't provide adequate direction for the facilitator.

Questioning. You don't want students engaging in practice before they are ready. The same principle applies to adults. Well-placed and effective questions, and the responses they elicit, can help you assess whether teachers are ready to proceed in the session. If they aren't ready, our facilitators know to go back and spend extra time on instruction. We follow the presentation of the knowledge and skills with a set of questions to check teachers' understanding of the material and clarify the message before proceeding to practice. Because they are adults and not students, we try to stay away from questions that are purely recall when possible.

- How will this teaching skill benefit you, the teacher?
- How will this teaching skill benefit students?
- Which step will be the hardest to execute?

Closing. At the end of the session, bring everyone back together to connect the dots, provide perspective on what has been accomplished, and invigorate the teachers to go forth and conquer.

First draft

If you have gone through the process above to create your outline, creating a first draft is straight forward. Use the outline and resources to develop a draft of the session in a presentation format such as PowerPoint by fleshing out bullet points and creating smooth transitions. The meat of the session should be present, but feel free to leave placeholders for visuals, formatting, or facilitator notes. Circulate it among the Professional Learning team, future facilitators, and any other qualified reviewers to gather notes to produce the final draft. Don't skip the feedback step. It is much better to hear a piece of critical feedback from a peer than to have that same piece of feedback be given to you 20 times from your 20 audience members as something that prevented them from fully engaging in your session.

Final draft

Once you're satisfied that the first draft is solid, add enough detail to the document so that you or another facilitator could use to present the material. If you are preparing this for someone else to deliver, or even if you will be delivering the session in later years, we recommend you include enough detail for them to internalize it without your help. This allows the facilitator to internalize the session on their own time without having to consult your calendar, as well as create a session that you can use in the future when you find similar gaps among your cohort of teachers. Include clear and complete notes for the facilitator that provide a script as well as the teacher-level outcomes that should be achieved by each section of the session, in case they choose to edit the script to make its facilitation comfortable. We will cover the actual internalization of a session in chapter 20. The final step of writing a session is to come back to the document after it has been delivered. Revisiting the final draft with feedback from teachers and facilitators in hand ensures that you make changes while the information is fresh in your head. The next time the session is delivered, the participants will benefit from this feedback. The feedback you record makes the next part of our process, revising and editing, much easier.

~ CHAPTER REFLECTION ~

1. We start by planning the practice portion of the session not because it is the most fun to plan, but because it is the important part of a professional learning experience. Which section of a session might be the most fun for you to plan, given your strengths and facilitation style? How can you structure your session writing process so that you maintain your focus on the importance of practice and give it the time it deserves?

2. What does the relationship between the timing of a session and the objective of a session mean for your individual context? How long are you usually given for professional learning opportunities with your cohort? How much content, then, can you feasibly tackle in an average session?

3. Where do your current strengths lie as a session writer? If you have never written a session from scratch before, what natural strengths might you be able to employ when it is time to do so?

Professional Learning Session Creation Checklist

VISION

- What is the teacher-level gap that this session is trying to close? What will it look like when this gap is closed?
- How long is allotted for this session?
- How much content can you feasibly cover given the time?

OBJECTIVES

- Is the objective aligned to the teacher-level gap?
- Is the objective skill-based?
- Is the objective manageable and able to be taught in the time allotted for the session?

PRACTICE

- What practice would give participants an opportunity to practice the skill being taught?
- Does the practice also give the facilitator the opportunity to see if objectives were met?
- Is the practice as genuine to the actual classroom experience as possible?

KEY POINTS

- What is the KNOWLEDGE necessary to engage in the practice that teachers need to hear and understand?
- What are the SKILLS necessary to engage in the practice that teachers will need to see modeled in some way (video, teacher-model, think-aloud, etc.)?
- Do teachers have a set of steps that they can refer back to when executing the skill?
- Is there extraneous information that is not necessary to engage in the practice that needs to be cut?
- If you are struggling to determine the key points, ask yourself "What", "How" "When" and "Who."

Professional Learning Session Creation Checklist

STRUCTURE

- What is the best way to structure the session?
- Consider your objective, practice, and key points when determining the structure.
- Examples:
  - Gradual Release: INM, Examples or model, practice (i.e. Proactive Expectations)
  - Chunked: INM and Practice is broken into multiple parts (i.e. Big 6)
  - Experiential: Participants experience the skills as students (i.e. 5-Step Lesson)

RATIONALE

- What mindsets might keep the participants from engaging with the key points of this session that should be addressed before the INM of the session?
- What mindsets can be addressed during the INM of the session?
- If you are struggling to determine the rationale, ask yourself, "Why is this important for teachers and for students?"

S.P.I.C.E.

- Consider where you can insert SPICE to increase engagement:
  - Story
  - Personal Experience
  - Inspiration
  - Challenging
  - Enthusiasm

Checks For Understanding

- When and where do you need to check for participant understanding?
- Determine when teachers will need internal and external processing opportunities.
- Consider the cognitive level of Checks For Understanding, application, and analysis often work best with adult learners.

19

CHAPTER 19 **Session Revising and Editing**

"I'm not a very good writer, but I'm an excellent rewriter."

— James A. Michener

One of the biggest benefits of spending a lot of time on the writing process and thinking through a session through the eyes of facilitators, participants, and students, is that over time you grow a library of sessions that have been written for your distinct audience. Because we at Teaching Excellence have had a dedicated Professional Learning team for 6 years, we don't write new sessions from scratch as often as we used to. Instead, we dust off sessions that were previously written and try to make each iteration of its delivery more effective than the previous. To do this, we not only have a process for writing sessions, but we also have a process for editing them to be presented again. There are levels to rewriting, from the global to the granular.

Revising vs. Editing

Revising involves looking at the session as a whole and rewriting entire sections, such as the key points, method of practice, timing or pacing, checks for understanding, questions, or even the structure of the session itself. Review and feedback from other team members typically precede the revision process, and the editor has some leeway in the execution of the rewrite. This typically happens when the need that a session is supposed to address is widely acknowledged, yet the session didn't hit the nail on the head.

Editing dials down into the details, such as grammar, punctuation, spelling, and formatting. It can focus on updating materials to using contemporary references. Often the editing process is formalized in a style guide, which can also include elements of branding, typeface, logos, and color palette. There is little room for preference in editing. While this happens to all sessions, regardless of the previous level of effectiveness, the most editing occurs with sessions that closed the teacher gap, but for which participants and/or facilitators gave a lot of critical feedback.

If you think of a session as a house, editing is cleaning, and revising is remodeling.

We spend time revising a session when we know the need for the session is there, but the session is not meeting the needs of our teachers as it is currently written. This part of the process, just as writing a session from scratch, can involve multiple drafts.

Catalysts and sources

Revision is part of the development of every session, but revising an existing session can be triggered and informed by several causes and sources.

Classroom data. In the role of teacher educator, you are uniquely situated to see how novice teachers implement the strategies conveyed in Professional Learning sessions and how the students respond. In addition to providing feedback to the teacher in terms of glows and grows, you can also bring that data back to the session writing process. Discussions with teachers and with other teacher educators can uncover trends that prompt a revision to address the reality in the classroom. If the session was successful, teachers replicate the practice in their classrooms. The pieces of the session that are missing from your observations of, and discussions with, teachers can indicate which portions of the sessions need more significant revision.

Session data. Gather input from each session to evaluate the material on clarity, relevance, engagement, and effectiveness. You want the teachers to leave prepared to implement the new strategies with their students. Also, get feedback from the facilitators to gauge ease of internalization, preparation, and presentation, and additionally to evaluate how the teachers received the content. We ask the same set of questions every time we present a session to allow us to compare quantitative data to other sessions and other times of the year, and to gather qualitative data about how being in the session felt to participants. We then use this data to guide future revisions.

Shifts in focus. As advances in education occur, strategies and tactics can change and sessions will require revision to update them to current practices. For example, at TE our session on checks for understanding (CFUs) focused on crafting aligned, rigorous checks for understanding and executing them consistently with all students. However, our scope and sequence for first-year teachers changed to focus on data analysis and assessment. We overhauled the session to accentuate data-driven CFUs. This revision required major changes to the key points, structure and practice of the session to incorporate a methodology for capturing, synthesizing and analyzing data from CFUs to make informed decisions about student progress.

Revision Process Checklist

When revising a session, you must set your sights on the big picture. It's too early to worry about typos or misplaced apostrophes. The paragraph in which they occur might be discarded or significantly rewritten. Below are the big categories

196

of edits that a session may need. You may find that some sessions need significant attention to many of these categories, while others may only need heavy lifting in one or two. You'll notice that the last step "Circle Back on Changes" is noted as "NECESSARY," as you will want to view the session holistically once any changes have been made to ensure that it still flows smoothly from beginning to end, given your new tweaks.

Session revision checklist	
New session and big-picture vision	What is the vision and/or outcome of your session? Has it changed since this session was last presented? Are there any big-picture considerations that affect this session?
My session ideas	How would I craft this session if I was starting from scratch? What would I include, and how would I make it interesting?
Vision gaps	How does the new vision differ from the old and what changes are required to span the gap?
Timing changes	Is the external time different from previous iterations? How should the session components be triaged? What can be allotted more time?
Structure	Are structural changes required? Is there sufficient emphasis on practice? Was practice successful the last time this session was presented?
Writing checklist items	Are any components missing from the writing checklist?
External facing – PPT	Does the PowerPoint enable novice teachers to process the key points?
External facing – Resources	Does the session require additional resources to help participants master the material?
Internal Facing - PPT	Have the facilitator notes been moved to the PowerPoint? Are they facilitator friendly?
NECESSARY: Circle back on changes	Does the session flow? Does it feel choppy and fragmented?

Editing

Whether or not a session needs serious revising, all sessions must be edited each time they are facilitated. Once the content is sound, the editor switches gears for the final edit. Editing can become tedious, but providing excellent and professional resources communicates to teachers that you value their time and their profession, and want to provide them with the highest quality materials.

The most important practice in editing is to slow down. As educators, plowing and skimming through mountains of material can become second nature. But skimming is exactly how typos are missed—the ones that are glaringly obvious once they're projected on a giant screen in a room full of teachers. Take time to read every word, running your finger along the line if necessary to keep you from sprinting ahead. It often helps to switch from your preferred reading platform (screen/print) to the other. Or do both.

We recommend that you pay close attention to a few things to ensure that your teachers focus on the material you are presenting and nothing else. Doing this will not only ensure that your materials look professional, but can also help you save time in future revising and editing processes.

Fonts. Settle on a standard typeface and font size for your organization and stick to it. We use separate fonts for body text , titles, and transition slides to make slides more appealing to the audience.

Branding. A consistent look and feel communicates that a thoughtful process and organization lies behind the document you have produced. We place our logo in the bottom right corner of every slide, exactly one pica from the edges. Never cover, move, or delete your program logo. Branding becomes branding only when it is consistent.

Spacing. When laying out a slide, pay careful attention to consistent spacing between objects. If there are three photos on a slide and the first two are 0.5" apart, then the third photo can't be 1.5" from the second. The message of quality and professionalism shouts from the details.

Spelling. Though spell and grammar check can be wonderful tools, they often miss small errors that only a human eye would notice. If you use graphics, such as SmartArt in PowerPoint, check all the text manually. Spell and grammar check don't check text within SmartArt.

Session Checklist

We use this checklist before we present a session to additional facilitators to assure that we have accounted for everything. If you write sessions only to deliver yourself, then this level of detail may not be necessary, though we still strongly recommend that you create a checklist for yourself as you go through this process.

Session review checklist	
Big Picture	1. Objective present 2. Big idea present 3. INM present 4. Practice present 5. Materials present 6. Times present 7. Closing present 8. CFUs present
Zoom-In: Content	*Introduction to New Material* 1. 1. Highlight changes (and duplicate in Facilitator Notes) 2. 2. Ensure clarity of content (do these key points make sense?) 3. 3. Verify that process makes sense *Practice & Application* 1. Highlight changes 2. Complete the practice (and check for clarity of instructions) *Timing & Pacing of Each Chunk of Session* 1. Times add up to the correct total 2. Times are accurate (+/- 1 minute)
Resource Sheet	1. Aligned to the PowerPoint 2. Tables are easy to read 3. Fonts are normed 4. Branding is consistent 5. Spacing (keep it consistent and allow room for writing on hard copies) 6. Spelling (certain features do not check your spelling - you must check manually)
PowerPoint	1. Aligned to the Resource Sheet (if there is one) 2. Visuals and Tables are the appropriate size (for reading across the room) 3. Fonts are normed 4. Branding is consistent 5. Spacing is consistent 6. Spelling has been checked

Roles and Responsibilities

To minimize the load on facilitators and to ensure consistency, the Professional Learning leadership team standardizes sessions. This frees facilitators to focus on internalizing the content of the session. Consider how you divide the work load between the different staff members who write and facilitate professional development in your specific context, and how different staff members can hold each other accountable for deadlines and outputs.

Session facilitators sometimes edit a session to incorporate a different method of explaining a key idea or a different method of practice. These one-off changes differ from facilitator to facilitator, usually in collaboration with the session writer/owner.

The revision/editing load is typically two to three sessions per month for each member of the Professional Learning leadership team, depending on the level of effort. A session owner charged with writing a new session for that month will have a lighter load where revision or editing is concerned.

During peak times, such as onboarding for summer induction, the Professional Learning leadership team might outsource revision to other team members, providing guidance and a framework for reference. A pre-meeting establishes the strengths (don't change) and weaknesses (please change) of a session, followed by milestones for reporting progress to ensure the quality of the revisions are on track to make the final product. When revisions are complete, the session owner uses the session editing checklist to ensure all the details are in place.

To keep the bar of quality high, the Professional Learning leadership team collaborates with content specialists and instructional leadership to align on our vision of an effective teacher and a rigorous classroom. This process includes gathering resources to share with novice teachers, presenting sessions especially tailored to their lesson planning track (5E, 5-Step, PDP), or grouping sessions by similar grade levels (ES/MS/HS) or contents (math, ELA, science, etc.).

Timeline

For each session, revision and edits should be finalized two to three weeks before the date of the session to allow facilitators to meet with the session writer/reviser, ask clarifying questions, discuss tweaks and have time to prepare and internalize the content.

You never want to feel as though this process is rushed, regardless of what your situation looks like, so make sure you budget time accordingly. We develop the onboarding and induction sessions in May to be presented the following summer. During the school year, as the Professional Learning team works on the four-week cycle discussed earlier, session writing, revision, and editing occur continuously. This cycle continues throughout the year, culminating with the final Professional Learning Saturday sessions in April.

If the purpose of the revising and editing process has been met, then regardless of whether you wrote a session from scratch or improved an existing session from your library, it is necessary to allow the ultimate facilitator to focus on getting ready to deliver the material.

~ CHAPTER REFLECTION ~

1. This book has regularly referenced the idea of a four-week timeline. While we have found this to be helpful, it is simply a result of our context. In what timeline will you usually be writing your sessions? When, then, should your session writing or editing process look like?

2. So much of a successful revision process relies on the incorporation of feedback from colleagues and participants. Do you currently have an effective method of obtaining feedback that enables you to make such revisions in the future? If not, what steps might you take to begin gathering more useful data moving forward?

3. Do you currently have a template, format, or brand that you rely on when creating or editing sessions? A one-time investment of time to create a template that can be used for all future sessions could not only save you tremendous amounts of time, but could also help set the tone for your audience in later professional learning settings.

20

CHAPTER 20 **Internalizing a Session**

> "It usually takes me more than three weeks to prepare for a good impromptu speech."
>
> — Mark Twain

You're in a room with two to three dozen teachers. All eyes are on you. Thirty to 90 minutes from now they will walk out with a new skill that will empower them to transform their classroom and measurably improve student outcomes.

The only way to make this time worthwhile for all involved—and to guide teachers in the practice of bringing excellence to the classroom—is to model the level of preparation required to deliver excellence. That is where internalization comes in.

Internalization is the process of memorizing, processing, and understanding the content and structure of a session to maximize participant mastery.

Excellence is not an accident

For any session to be successful, clear, and engaging, you must have a thorough understanding of the pedagogical basis and optimum flow of the session.

Pedagogy. Most Professional Learning sessions present best practices for classroom culture or instructional planning and delivery. To effectively present a session, you must be prepared to speak at length and in depth about the topic extemporaneously (relatively independent of your notes), as your audience will likely ask questions as they attempt to apply the lessons to their own setting. The first time you present any session, you will likely need to do some outside reading and brushing up on the techniques covered in the session.

The Teaching Excellence Professional Learning team supports a variety of grade levels and content areas. We work with teachers from Pre-K to 12th grade covering content areas from core subjects such as math and science to electives such as orchestra, art, yoga, and dance teachers. As a result, our facilitators must be prepared to target widely varying strategies to address the range of ages and content. Even if you are presenting to your own grade level and content, it is important to re-familiarize yourself with the focus of the session.

As our program has grown, we have endeavored to group together teachers with common teaching assignments. However, this has not always been the case for us, and we continually find that we must think through our sessions from multiple angles. This will be especially true if you are campus-based and facilitate to teachers across grade levels and contents. For example, while a session on teacher modeling and think-alouds might have universal application, as you walk through the internalization process, you should brainstorm examples to apply the skill to a variety of classrooms to meet the needs of all participants in your session.

Flow. Once you can articulate the key ideas of a session in a clear and engaging way, shift your focus to the flow of the session. Consider everything from the logistics of providing materials to the pacing for processing and practice. Stumbling through practical-level details is a sure sign of lack of preparation. It can be helpful to sketch out the different pieces of a session and how they drive toward the ultimate outcome.

The Internalization Process

Internalization involves a well-defined set of steps implemented over a number of days or weeks. We use a four-week period to maximize the success of the session. This structured process includes: giving facilitators time to read, discuss, and ask clarifying questions; allowing facilitators to watch the session writer model hotspots (challenging segments); and practicing the session. The advantage of doing all of this is that it enables to you stand in front of a room of teachers with the confidence that not only can you articulate the knowledge and skills necessary for success, but you can also handle questions, pushback, or hesitation from teachers to guide all participants toward more effective teaching. Facilitators internalize sessions so that they are able to deliver the content with fidelity to the original vision.

The Schedule

Below is a typical four-week run-up to a Professional Learning Saturday from the perspective of our facilitators; we saw a similar schedule earlier from the perspective of the writer. The schedule is framed in terms of sessions you receive from someone else, whether a member of your team or another professional who has shared the content with you. If you have written a session to facilitate yourself, the process below can be sped up a bit, but all components should still be accounted for.

Week 1. As a facilitator, you receive your session assignment and read through it on your own, focusing on outcomes, key points, practice, and structure. As soon as possible, send any clarifying questions or feedback to the session writer, or record them for yourself so that changes any changes can be implemented before week two.

Week 2. Meet with the writer or another qualified peer to walk through the finalized version of the session, focusing on hotspots or areas with the potential to confuse the participants. After the meeting, revisit and rehearse the focus areas and internalize the hotspots and timing.

Week 3. The content should be static at this point. Meet with the writer, who will model the trickiest parts of the session. You can also ask a facilitation or content expert to help you think through these parts of the session. You might want to make small edits or changes to tailor the content to the concerns of the audience for this specific session and to personalize it with stories and humor to engage the participants.

Week 4. Meet with the writer to practice a dry run of a critical portion of the session and receive feedback either from the writer or a peer.

In week three or four, facilitators schedule a one-on-one meeting with the member of the Professional Learning team who is serving as their facilitation coach to discuss hotspots, SPICE strategies (Stories, Personal Experience, Inspiration, Challenge, Enthusiasm)

The Process

As you work through the four-week schedule, you should hit these critical points.

Identify major outcomes. Familiarize yourself with the major overview and desired outcomes of the session so you know where you want teachers to be by the end of the time. Identify and absorb:

- The objectives
- The big idea
- The knowledge and skills that teachers will master

Establish the details. Clarify how you will address these elements and engage the participants regarding:

- Communicating and modeling the key points
- Creating opportunities for processing the content and checks for understanding
- Practice
- Closing

Connect details to outcome. Ask yourself, "How does each section of this session connect to the objectives and big idea?"

Personalize the delivery. Go through the session notes and change the language to resonate naturally with your voice. If the session doesn't have transitions that reflect your perspective, return to your notes about connections and use them to draft your own transitions.

Practice out loud. Use your script to focus on communicating all the points of the session and making smooth transitions.

Spice it up. Add or flesh out SPICE strategies that engage the teachers and better connect the chunks to the outcomes and big idea.

Practice out loud. Again, including the SPICE strategies.

Practice with times and materials. If the session doesn't already have milestones scheduled on a timeline, create them. Focus on sticking to the times and practice disseminating materials or asking teachers to access materials during the session. For example, if you want teachers to take out a lesson plan, you should rehearse waiting for them to locate the necessary materials.

Practice until a glance will suffice. Just as practice is the foundation of student learning and teacher skill, it's also the foundation for a successful session. Practice until you can facilitate with an occasional glance at your notes to guide you through the transitions. Our veteran facilitators sum up each section of the session with a word or a phrase written in the margin of their notes in large print. When facilitating, a quick glance that these words and phrases is all they need to catapult them into the next section of their session. This can occur only when the requisite amount of internalization has happened. If you need the notes for the actual delivery of the session, you aren't ready yet. Once you can communicate the same information in several different ways and sound as though you aren't reading off a script, the internalization process is complete.

~ CHAPTER REFLECTION ~

1. What, in your mind, is the biggest difference between a public speaker and a facilitator?

2. How dependent are you on your notes when you speak in front of a large audience? Do you glance down at your prepared remarks only occasionally or are you virtually reading from a script? What does this say about your flexibility to adjust course during a session or about the effectiveness of your current internalization process?

3. Given your answer to the previous question, which step in the internalization process would you consider to be a strength? Which step would you consider your greatest focus area for your next facilitation opportunity?

21

Facilitating a Session

Lecturing. Speaking about topic with a focus on clarity of information.

Presenting. Speaking about a topic with a focus on clarity of information and engagement of the participants.

Facilitation. Controlling the learning experience with a focus on clarity of the information, engagement of the participants, and application of the skill with an overarching goal of participant mastery.

All too often, those charged with conveying information or teaching a skill to others fail to view themselves as facilitators of that knowledge or skill. At TE, we focus on facilitation that empowers teachers to apply a specific strategy to their practice. Lecturing and presenting perform the essentials of transfer of information, but do not adequately prepare teachers to execute changes in their classrooms. If we do our jobs as facilitators with a high degree of skill, our teachers are engaged, and the focus of the session remains on the objectives to be covered. Exemplary facilitation incorporates all three elements.

Expedience = Clearly deliver key points. Our teachers attend training on Saturday and return to the classroom on Monday. They have to be able to turn around a new skill almost immediately. This context engenders a sense of urgency—an urgency we expect novice teachers to catch and apply in their own classrooms—to cover the material quickly and explain how to improve as clearly as possible.

Expectations = Engage the participants in the topic. Our teachers face the high expectations placed on first-year teachers. They are frequently exhausted and overwhelmed with to-do lists and next steps. We make our sessions engaging to hold their attention and make the most of their time. This tightrope act focuses on the material covered with the expectation that actively engaged teachers are more likely to implement the strategies we cover.

Mastery = Require teachers to apply the skills. Most importantly, teachers need skills they can execute in their classrooms immediately. We schedule time to practice those skills because practice with colleagues and facilitators is more effective at cementing skills than trying out a new skill for the first time in front of students on Monday morning. Our experience shows that trial runs and quick feedback during Professional Learning sessions increase the likelihood of success when implementing the skills in the classroom.

The result of maximizing these three elements is that teachers leave Professional Learning sessions with the ability to execute the skills in their classes immediately.

Teaching Excellence Facilitation Excellence Rubric

When our Professional Learning team was in its infancy, those charged with developing other facilitators struggled with coaching members of the team to better outcomes. We lacked the common vocabulary and vision necessary to make dialogues and development possible. We had access to tools for developing public speakers, but those resources were focused on the presenter, not on the outcomes for the participants. Presentation skills are surely an essential element in developing a strong facilitator, but conveying knowledge and building skill in an audience goes beyond developing an engaging presence.

Over the course of two years, we created the Teaching Excellence Facilitation Excellence Rubric (TEFER), which conveys the essential elements a facilitator should embody. The TEFER is the backbone of facilitation at Teaching Excellence. Our facilitators are coached through, and evaluated against, this rubric throughout the year.

We created this tool more as a rubric rather than a checklist to allow team members to use it as a development tool, with or without the support of a facilitation coach. The various columns display participant actions that the facilitator or an observer might see, as well as some actions that the facilitator could take to improve participant outcomes. The categories on the TEFER in the "Mastery" column summarize the characteristics of a strong facilitator. The goal for facilitators is to move along the continuum until they are consistently demonstrating the elements in the "Mastery" column of the rubric, therefore increasing participant mastery, teacher practice and, ultimately, student outcomes.

This section briefly explains each indicator of the rubric (from the most foundational to the most advanced) and provides a rationale as to how the rubric plays a role in the facilitation of a strong adult learning experience.

Facilitator presence

Approaching Proficiency	Proficient	Mastery
• Inconsistently displays a professional and engaging presence throughout session • Tone or presence lack confidence, warmth, and/or respect • Tone or presence appears patronizing, cocky, or distant at times • Over-explains at times throughout the session • Presence of distracting anchor word and/or verbal tick • Norms are not addressed or enforced in the presence of unfocused behavior • Facilitator is completely stationary or movement throughout the session and/or gestures are distracting (pacing, nervous shifting, unnecessary or confusing gestures, etc.)	• Consistently exemplifies a professional and engaging presence throughout session • Tone is generally warm, respectful, and communicates confidence facilitating for adults • Word choice is generally efficient with no distracting anchor words or verbal ticks • Norms are explicitly set and enforced throughout the session • Gestures and movement throughout the session and placement in the room are not distracting and do not detract from the session	• Consistently exemplifies a professional and engaging presence throughout all interactions during PLS • Tone is consistently warm, respectful, and communicates confidence facilitating for adults • Word choice is consistently efficient with no anchor words or verbal ticks • Norms are appropriately enforced; participant engagement eliminates the need for proactively setting norms (You're a facilitation stud and no one would dare...) • Gestures and movement throughout the session and placement in the room are purposeful, effective, and enhance the session

While the star of any session should be the content, not the facilitator, the words and actions of a strong facilitator can add to participant engagement and mastery. The "Proficient" column reflects actions that allow the session to be facilitated as written. Any action that takes focus away from the session or makes the material more difficult to understand would fall in the left-hand column, and those words and actions that enhance the quality of the session for its participants fall in the right-hand column. Some of our newer teacher educators find it challenging to master the right tone for adults. Many teacher educators accustomed to speaking to students have the tendency to use the same inflection and word choice with adults. Adults pick up on this tone and take offense to being treated as students. Engagement increases as facilitators learn the right register and tone to use with adults.

Use of time

Approaching Proficiency	Proficient	Mastery
• Not all planned and necessary activities are accomplished due to inefficient use of time • Time is lost due to mismanagement of materials/resources within facilitator's locus of control • Uses time inefficiently or adds unnecessary disruption when presented with unforeseen occurrences	• All planned and necessary activities are executed • Facilitator has prepared materials/resources for the flow of the session	• Participant mastery is maximized due to the decisions made by the facilitator • Facilitator has prepared materials/resources for the flow of the session and any unforeseen occurrences are handled without unnecessary attention and a minimum of disruption

This rubric row highlights the importance of letting the content remain center stage throughout the learning experience and is designed to help prepare a facilitator for their assigned session. For a facilitator to score high on this indicator, they must have internalized the flow of the session well enough to make seamless use of all materials and ensure that each chunk of the session receives its due time. A masterful facilitator can achieve session outcomes despite unforeseen circumstances.

Sense of urgency

Approaching Proficiency	Proficient	Mastery
• Rationale and/or importance for the topic is absent or communicated ineffectively • Transitions appear unplanned and/or disrupt the flow the session • Delivery of instructions is repetitive or unclear, resulting in many participant questions	• Rationale and/or importance for the topic is referenced at the beginning of the session • Transitions are executed smoothly in a way that does not disrupt the flow of the session • Clearly and efficiently communicates instructions to maximize practice time and proactively addresses confusion	• Rationale and/or importance for the topic is regularly referenced throughout the session and includes multiple examples (data, research, student connections, stories, etc.) • Transitions are executed smoothly, bridging prior learning and the session's objectives to upcoming activities • Clearly and efficiently communicates instructions and rationale to maximize practice time and proactively address confusion

Sense of urgency is related to the use of time, but we believe it warrants its own row as the nuance often comes up in conversations with facilitators. Use of time ensures that every activity in a session is given the appropriate amount of time. Sense of urgency ensures that the purpose of each of these chunks is clear to, and achieved by, participants. Instructions should be clear and allow participants to fully engage in the practice. The rationale should apply to a wide variety of teachers to sufficiently invest them in the session outcomes such that they authentically engage with all practice opportunities.

Approaching Proficiency	Proficient	Mastery
• Presenter appears uncomfortable with session material (reads notes as if they are a script, unsure of key points) • Facilitator makes little or no attempt to anticipate or address misunderstandings or previous mindset issues • Key points are alluded to but lack clarity and consistency • Facilitator model is either lacking or ineffective • Session facilitation lacks connections throughout the session or may do so ineffectively	• Presenter appears comfortable with session material (not overly reliant on notes or unsure of key points) • Facilitator has anticipated some misunderstandings or previous mindset issues and makes attempt to address them. Key points are referenced in the session in a succinct or consistent manner • Facilitator effectively models the content of the session but may not make this model explicit or model at all appropriate times • Facilitator occasionally creates connections throughout the session (among key points, stories, examples, etc.) to solidify learning and engagement	• Presenter is comfortable with session material (facilitator is confident enough to facilitate without notes and has clear key points) • Facilitator has anticipated several misunderstandings or previous mindset issues and effectively addresses them • Key points are referenced throughout the session in a succinct and consistent manner • Facilitator effectively and explicitly models the content of the session at appropriate times • Facilitator regularly and effectively creates connections throughout the session (among key points, stories, examples, etc.) to solidify learning and engagement

When facilitators have become proficient with these skills, they are prepared to deliver clear content to participants. As you can see in this row, the bullet points not only allow Professional Learning team members to evaluate facilitators, but they are worded so that facilitators themselves can better internalize a session independent of any support. Teacher educators without a dedicated Professional earning team can evaluate and coach themselves as they determine whether they are ready to deliver a session to a room of teachers.

At TE, we regularly employ the Facilitator Model, meaning that we model for our teachers the skill being taught. We explicitly bring this to the attention of the teachers so that they are aware of the model both in content and execution so they can take note and implement it. For example, if a facilitator uses several quality questioning strategies in a session on increasing student processing opportunities, but does not call these out explicitly, then participants might not make the connection on their own or replicate the practice in their own class. When facilitating a session on incorporating a skill in lesson planning, the facilitator would demonstrate their thought process in a think-aloud as they work through the appropriate portion of that session.

Checks for understanding and questioning

Approaching Proficiency	Proficient	Mastery
• Participants are given few opportunities to answer CFUs • CFUs posed to participants are not aligned with the objectives of the session • Questioning techniques do not engage most participants	• Participants are given many opportunities to answer aligned CFUs • Questioning techniques encourage all participants to engage	• Participants are given many opportunities to answer aligned CFUs at a variety of cognitive levels • Questioning techniques require all participants to engage • Questions are consistently open-ended to increase participant engagement and ownership of content

We ensure that teachers have several opportunities to process the new information we present. Further, we strive to make sure these opportunities are available to all teachers and structured in a way that encourages or requires all teachers to engage with them. Questions should be structured to allow participants to demonstrate their understanding, rather than simply repeating key information from the session. If there is only one right answer to a question, it is usually a question that we discard. The quality of teacher response offers important data to the facilitator about how well the session material engages and resonates with the participants. Facilitators can use this information to make in-the-moment decisions to ensure practice opportunities maximize mastery.

Facilitator/participant interaction

Approaching Proficiency	Proficient	Mastery
• Facilitator does not effectively build relationships with participants in sessions • Facilitator does not attempt to use a SPICE (Stories, Personal Experience, Inspiration, Challenge, Enthusiasm) strategy or does so ineffectively • Facilitator responds to unplanned input, difficult questions, or participant pushback in a way that devalues the input or participant • Facilitator responds to unplanned input, difficult questions, or participant pushback in a way that negatively impacts mastery of content (contradictions, failure to use right-is-right, unspecific or general response) • Facilitator does not make any adjustments to increase energy and engagement when necessary	• Actively seeks to build relationships with participants in sessions by using names and providing positive praise • Facilitator effectively uses a SPICE strategy to increase engagement and buy-in for the material of the session • Facilitator respectfully responds to unplanned input, difficult questions, and participant pushback • Mastery of content is not affected by unplanned input, difficult questions, or participant pushback, though it may affect the flow or pacing of the session Facilitator effectively reads the mood of the room and makes accommodations related to energy and engagement of participants • Facilitator attempts to create a shared ownership of the learning with participants (throws questions back to audience, asks for opinions, asking open-ended questions or questions without correct answers)	• Facilitator values the experiences of participants by referencing campus observations and previous participant discussions • Facilitator effectively uses a variety of strategically chosen SPICE strategies throughout the session to maximize engagement and buy-in • Facilitator respectfully responds to unplanned input, difficult questions, and participant pushback in a way that does not affect pacing or mastery of content • Facilitator effectively reads the mood of the room and makes accommodations related to energy and engagement of participants as well as increasing equity of voice • Facilitator attempts to create a shared ownership of learning with participants (participants provide opinions, answer, and pose questions to each other; overwhelming majority of participants engage in session, final word comes from teacher)

Facilitators can focus on this indicator only when they have mastered the others. They must be sufficiently comfortable with the content and flow of the session to allow themselves to deviate from the script as they see fit to maximize both engagement and mastery. In sessions with 30 or more participants, all teaching different content at different campuses, this skill is a non-negotiable if a facilitator on Saturday hopes to influence teacher actions come Monday morning. Our facilitators develop the ability to respond to an unplanned question through extensive practice, following the principles indicated below.

Questions applicable to all	Questions applicable to 1 participant only	Question indicates lack of understanding of concept or potentially dangerous mindset.
• Efficiently answer the question, connecting your response to the key points of the session. Ask original participant, and the room, if the clarification has helped.	• Thank them for the question and let them know that you will revisit this with them during the work time. Never fail to do this if you have promised it!	• Look at the clock, as this may require you to readjust time in the session. • If you're struggling to find the right words, throw it out to the group ("It seems like some people want to respond to this. What do you think?") • If the issue is a lack of understanding, ensure that the confusion is addressed so that other participants are clear.

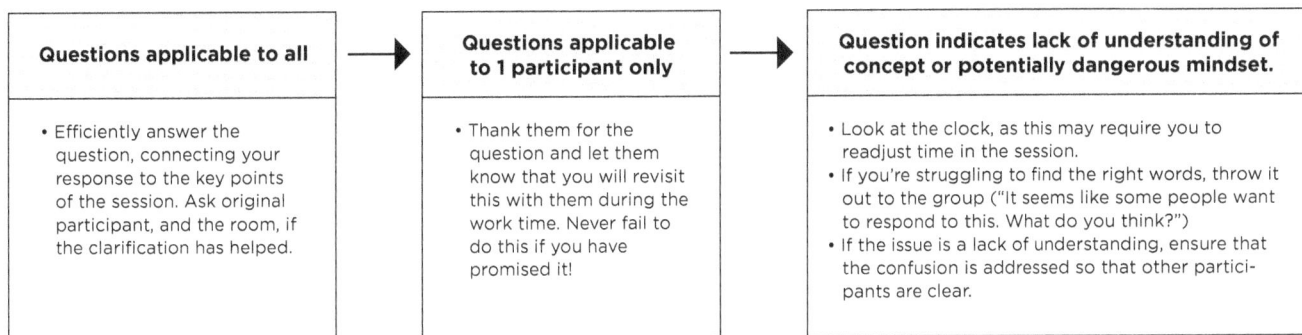

Participant mastery

Approaching proficiency	Proficient	Mastery
• Participants are not actively engaged in practice or are practicing incorrectly without being supported • Time spent listening to the facilitator is greater than time spent with participants engaging with key points • Participants do not attempt to create next steps or are not given the time to do so • Group reflections and share-outs do not focus on key points	• Facilitator circulates during practice and ensures that all participants are actively engaged • Significantly more session time is spent on participant engagement with the key points than is spent listening to the facilitator • Participants are given reflection time to create aligned next steps based on the key points of the session • Group reflections and share-outs are facilitated in a way that focuses on the key points of the session	• Facilitator circulates during practice and provides feedback to groups or individuals that is aligned to the objectives of the session • Significantly more session time is spent on a variety of participant engagement strategies (engaging with colleagues, reflections, role plays, planning, reading, etc.) with the key points than is spent listening to the facilitator • Participants create aligned next steps and are given the space to commit to action (put in a lesson plan, tell a neighbor, put on a post-it, etc.) • Group reflections and share-outs are facilitated to ensure all participants engage with key take-aways

At this point, a facilitator truly begins to evaluate how well participants are mastering the content of a session. Many facilitators believe they are *on* only while delivering content at the beginning of sessions or explaining activities and their connection to the objectives. While content delivery has a significant impact on the later actions of participants, the actions listed in this row represent how a facilitator can impact the mastery of teachers throughout *all* portions of a session. Skillful facilitators can push teachers to achieve the outcome of the session during all times that they are together. That way, when teachers implement the skills on Monday, they have done enough work beforehand to perform well in front of students.

Spending time digesting the language in the "Mastery" column of this rubric clarifies the true power a well-written session can hold as well as the art and science involved in becoming an exemplary facilitator. We developed this tool as a means of helping both individuals and teams hone their practice, and it is our hope that it will be useful in your own development as a facilitator as well. The next chapter will cover how we develop our teacher educators as facilitators using this rubric as well as several other structures.

~ CHAPTER REFLECTION ~

1. What, in your mind, is the greatest difference between a public speaker and a facilitator? After digesting the content of this chapter, has your answer changed since the last time you answered this question?

2. Think back to a recent session in which you either facilitated or participated. Did each section of that session contribute to the participants' ultimate mastery of the objective?

3. Think about your time in the classroom with students. What was your favorite part? The part that gave you the most excitement and energy? Where does that skill live on this rubric? How can you use that skill in your work facilitating learning experiences for adults?

22

CHAPTER 22 **Developing Facilitators**

Teaching Excellence is built on a core principle of continuous improvement that applies to every level, from the teacher engaged in the classroom to the teacher educator to the facilitators on the Professional Learning team. Consequently, we created a structure to support continuous improvement for facilitators through coaching and evaluation from the Professional Learning leadership team. This coaching includes feedback and evaluation on facilitation clarity, engagement, and application to ensure consistent excellence across the facilitation of all our sessions.

Program Structure

The Professional Learning leadership team leads, creates, and plans all facilitator training and serves as facilitator coaches. At Teaching Excellence, facilitator development has three components: onboarding, group sessions, and one-on-one coaching. Each is informed by data and the common goal of accelerating facilitator, and therefore teacher development.

Professional Learning Onboarding

The first opportunity for our Professional Learning team to develop facilitators is through onboarding each summer. This orientation, which occurs after our new teacher educators are hired and before our new teacher induction every summer, introduces facilitators to the basics of the best practices necessary to ensure consistent facilitation across all sessions. In two weeks of training, Professional Learning onboarding prepares the entire team for the general logistics, schedule, and content of the upcoming teacher onboarding while simultaneously delivering foundational facilitation skills and best practices to our new hires. Specific topics covered during this time include best practices for session internalization and facilitation, both covered in previous chapters. New teacher educators also get to participate in a model session acting as teachers. All new and returning facilitators attend onboarding for different lengths of time based on experience.

Group Sessions

Training throughout the year focuses on areas of need across the team based on observations during sessions, as well as teacher feedback from the sessions. These group sessions occur during our regular, weekly team meetings and are written using the same structure described in Chapter 18 on session writing. In these sessions, we explain the gap, why it's a problem, what it looks like, how to fix it, and provide time for our team to practice.

For example, in years when we have a larger percentage of new staff members, it is not uncommon for us to notice that our survey feedback contains many responses that indicate that our participants feel like they are not being treated as professionals. A session targeting this gap will share this data, give examples of what this gap looks like in sessions, and give facilitators some strategies to use in their sessions instead to make their participants feel like colleagues and professionals. This session would occur in the interim between Saturday trainings.

One-on-one Coaching

For the academic year, all full-time facilitators are assigned a coach from the Professional Learning team. The coach mentors facilitators, helps in internalizing Professional Learning sessions, and serves as the facilitator's evaluator. New facilitators are evaluated on the Teaching Excellence Facilitation Excellence Rubric and are rated each semester.

Individual coaching sessions focus on areas for improvement based on evaluations from facilitator coaches and survey feedback from participants. All facilitators are assigned a facilitation coach at the beginning of the year, and we believe that this consistency between coach and facilitator accelerates the growth of the team member.

At Teaching Excellence, a 30- to 45-minute check-in meeting with a facilitation coach and the facilitator is scheduled in the week prior to a Professional Learning Saturday. During these meetings, the coach can address hotspots (difficult portions of the session) or answer relevant questions. Coaches also help the facilitator to identify focus areas for development based on their progress as guided by the elements of the TEFER.

Facilitators then practice delivering a five- to ten-minute section of the session to the coach and receive feedback. Before our Professional Learning team was large enough to provide monthly feedback, individual facilitators used participant surveys, video observations, and notes from other team members to help them identify focus areas for themselves to prioritize as they facilitated future sessions.

Coaches observe facilitators at most but not all Professional Learning events, sometimes to provide feedback and other times to perform an evaluation. During the delivery of sessions, facilitators are completely focused on facilitation. Facilitation coaches observe and evaluate facilitators. At the end of a Professional Learning event, the participants complete a survey about the clarity and engagement of the facilitation and their confidence level of implementing the key skills from the session. Facilitators receive the qualitative and quantitative data from these surveys five days after delivering a session and observation notes or evaluations from the facilitation coaches. Facilitators reflect and review the data and discuss their reflection in their next facilitation coach check-in.

During the year, facilitation coaches also share trends they have observed to inform upcoming facilitator training sessions. Facilitation professional development takes place on an as needed basis usually happening approximately monthly throughout the school year.

We have found this to be an effective way to accelerate the development of team members as facilitators and, because it meets facilitators where they are and pushes them along a continuum of development, we have found this to be true regardless of their previous level of delivering adult learning experiences.

~ CHAPTER REFLECTION ~

1. If you are in a position to develop the facilitation ability of others, which of these structures would be easiest for you to implement on a short timeline? What would be the benefit to your team of doing so?

2. If you are not directly responsible for the facilitation development of others, how can you set up these structures in such a way that you and your colleagues benefit? Perhaps you could start mentoring opportunities, coach each other or set up opportunities provide feedback to one another on your sessions and facilitation.

Closing Thoughts

What brought you to teaching? Love of knowledge? Love of students? A desire to be a force for change in the world? All of the above?

As you take this step out of the classroom and into coaching, think back to the beginning of your journey. The same passion that inspired your first step can provide motivation as you extend your reach to foster positive change in student outcomes on a greater scale. In fact, holding onto that passion is essential for your success, the success of your teachers, and the success of the students.

As we discussed in this book, mindset is a foundational element to effectiveness. The mindset of a coach is other-focused, committed to enabling others to strive for (and achieve) excellence. The stakes are too high to relax into a drop-by-the-room-and-check-the-box mentality. Coaching is a holistic practice. You must bring your whole self to the table, engage with others, authentically build relationships, carefully observe and thoughtfully consider each step in the path down which you are guiding your teachers. By bringing your knowledge, skills, and experience to the world of your cohort of teachers, you will discern the needs of the students and the key lever required at any given moment to develop teachers who recognize and respond effectively to those needs.

While a certain amount of organization, management and administration is required to facilitate your effectiveness, the real impact of your work is in the key role of coaching teachers at the beginning of their careers, the point where you can make the biggest difference. By adopting the beliefs and implementing the strategies outlined in this book, over each academic year you will have the satisfaction of facilitating a rising trajectory in the competence and effectiveness of teachers, regardless of their starting point.

That's what coaching does—it transforms talent.

We condensed a year's worth of training and development into these pages; the training that all new instructional coaches at YES Prep receive during their first year working on the Teaching Excellence team.

We hope that in this book you found not only the knowledge of how to coach teachers, but also the inspiration to strive for excellence in yourself and your teachers, and a renewed energy to go the distance. We offer it as a starting point and also a reference to which you and your teachers can return to seek clarity, research ideas, find new ways to motivate your teachers to invest in key levers, solve a problem you can't crack, or simply power through the awkwardness that can arise during practice prior to seeing a teacher try a new skill in the classroom.

In your new role as a teacher educator, the breadth of your impact on student outcomes will increase exponentially. Each teacher you develop will instruct dozens or hundreds of students each year. Year after year, the work you do will affect the educational trajectory of thousands of students.

It is an honor and a joy that we find both humbling and rewarding. We are excited to welcome you to our ranks.

If you get the chance, come visit us in Houston to share the highs and lows of your experiences and collaborate on strategies to improve your coaching. Together we will accelerate the impact teachers have on students, joined in the effort of making the world a better place, one teacher and student at a time.